Canciones De Nuestra Cabaña

World Association
of Girl Guides and Girl Scouts

Nuestra Cabaña
Apartado Postal 406
Cuernavaca, Morelos, Mexico.

Published for the World Association of Girl Guides
and Girl Scouts by Girl Scouts of the U.S.A.

Printed in the United States of America
ISBN 0-88441-366-7
8   7   6   5   4

Contents

Camp-fire Openings and Greetings

Apertura Fogatas y Cantos de Bienvenida

Festivals and Ceremonies

Festivales y Ceremonias

Graces

Acciones de Gracias

Rounds and Canons

Rondas y Canones

Singing Games and Action Songs

Cantos-Juegos y Cantos con Movimientos

Part Songs

Cantos a dos o más voces

Vespers and Closings

Oraciones de la tarde y Cantos de Clausura

Other Favourites

Otros Favoritos

Preámbulo

Con nuestro agradecimiento ofrecemos *Canciones de Nuestra Cabaña* a ustedes, Guías/Scouts del mundo. Con agradecimiento porque gracias a la generosidad de músicos y compositores, propietarios de derechos de autor y Asociaciones Nacionales, esta recopilación es de y para todas nosotras.

Nos hemos esforzado en localizar y dar crédito a los propietarios de derechos de autor. Si hemos cometido algún error, pedimos acepten nuestras disculpas y con gusto haremos las correcciones necesarias en futuras ediciones.

Entre las muchas personas que han contribuido en esta tarea, en primer lugar demos las gracias a nuestra recopiladora la Srita. Hettie Smith. Su gran cariño por la música y por Nuestra Cabaña le han inspirado para beneficio nuestro. Estamos también muy agradecidas a la Srita. Winifred Hunt por su valiosa cooperación y gran esfuerzo en buscar los originales y conseguir los permisos. Nuestro más profundo agradecimiento a las Girl Scouts de los Estados Unidos por su valiosa colaboración.

Finalmente estamos en deuda con aquellos amigos de Nuestra Cabaña que con su fe y generosidad iniciaron este proyecto.

Comité de Nuestra Cabaña

Foreword

With gratitude we present *Canciones de Nuestra Cabaña* to you, Girl Guides and Girl Scouts of the world. With gratitude because, thanks to the generosity of individual musicians and songwriters, copyright owners and national associations, this collection is of, from, and for, all of us.

We have done our best to trace and credit copyright ownership. If we have erred, we ask acceptance of our apologies and information so that corrections may be made in future editions.

Among the many who have contributed to this endeavor, first thanks must go to Hettie Smith, our compiler. Her passion for music and her love for Our Cabaña inspired her efforts on our behalf. We are especially grateful to Winifred Hunt whose untiring help in searching out sources and in securing permission was invaluable. Our deep appreciation goes to Girl Scouts of the U.S.A. for their guidance and staff work. We have drawn on their expertise throughout the venture. Finally, we are greatly indebted to those friends of Our Cabaña whose faith and generosity initiated the project.

Our Cabaña Committee

Preludio

Al incorporarme inicialmente como líder a las actividades de las Girl Scouts, inmediatamente me impresionó la excelente calidad de su programa musical, el alto nivel del canto, así como la coleccion de canciones propias y encantadoras que descubrí en las publicaciones de las Girl Guides y Girl Scouts de Europa, Inglaterra y los Estados Unidos de América.

La importancia del canto en nuestro programa constituye uno de sus focos más importantes. De todas las artes, la música es la de mayor atracción universal. Y en toda música el canto constituye la forma fundamental y de mayor fuerza. Posee el poder de levantar el espíritu humano, de fomentar mayor comprensión, de fortalecer lazos comunes reforzando así los propósitos de nuestra organización. La música es nuestra organización. La música es nuestro idioma internacional. Valiéndonos de las riquezas de diversas culturas y tradiciones nos acercamos a todas en una hermandad internacional.

Acogemos esta colección de canciones nuevas sabiendo que serán ampliamente utilizadas y disfrutadas.

Clementine M. Tangeman

Prelude

Coming to Girl Scouting first as a leader, I was immediately impressed by the excellent quality of its music program, by the high standards of singing, and the discriminating and charming collections of songs I discovered among Girl Guide and Girl Scout Publications from Europe, the U.K., and the U.S.A.

The importance of singing in our program is one of its greatest strengths. Of all the arts, music has the most universal appeal. And in all music, singing is its most fundamental and powerful form. It has the power to lift the human spirit, to promote greater understanding, to strengthen common bonds, and thus to undergird the purposes of our movement. Music is our international language. Drawing on the rich resources of many cultures and traditions, it brings us all together in one worldwide sisterhood.

We welcome this fresh collection of songs, knowing that it will be widely used and enjoyed.

Clementine M. Tangeman

Nota de la Recopiladora

Antes de iniciar mis "notas" desearía expresar mi sincero agradecimiento a tantas personas cuyos nombres no puedo enumerar, pero especialmente a la Sra. Howard Katzenberg, Presidenta del Comité de Nuestra Cabaña, por su incansable labor y apoyo durante la recopilación de este cancionero.

Dentro de las siguientes páginas yo espero que ustedes puedan encontrar algo apropiado a todos los gustos y edades; para el campamento más alegre o el momento guía más inspirado, así como para la reunión semanal.

Algunas sugerencias para sacar el mejor provecho de este cancionero:

A las guiadoras que no se sienten muy seguras musicalmente:

a) Pidan ayuda a las guías con capacidad musical, quienes contando con su apoyo entusiasta y crítica constructiva pueden hacer maravillas.

b) Soliciten ayuda de sus amigas dentro y fuera del movimiento que les guste la música. Escojan a las más alegres.

A todas:

Utilicen a guitarristas para apoyar a sus cantantes, pero recuerden que muchas canciones salen mejor sin ningún acompañamiento.

Gocen creando instrumentos de percusión, pero eviten utilizarlos en tal forma que no se escuche la melodía.

Para relajarse inventen aplausos o porras, pero establezcan reglas de canto en su tropa o compañía en donde no tengan cabida los gritos.

(continuación en siguiente pagina)

Compiler's Notes

Before starting my notes, I would like to record my grateful thanks to so many people whom I cannot mention by name, but in particular to Mrs. Howard Katzenberg, chairman of Our Cabaña Committee, for her untiring work and support during the compiling of this songbook.

Within the following pages I hope that you can find something to suit all tastes and ages, the liveliest camp or most thoughtful Guides'/Scouts' Own Service, as well as the weekly meeting.

Here are a few hints on how to get the best out of this collection.

To leaders who feel musically unsure:

a) Do make use of musical troop members who, with your enthusiasm and helpful criticism, can do wonders.

b) Do call upon musical friends, within the movement and outside, but choose those with a sense of fun!

To all:

Use guitarists to support your singers, but remember that many songs are better with no accompaniment at all.

Have fun creating homemade percussion instruments but never use them so that the tune is "drowned"!

To "let off steam," make up yells or chants, but set a standard of singing in your troop in which shouting has no place at all.

May the music in your program grow in verve, vigour, and variety, but above all in enjoyment.

Hettie G. Smith

Nota de la
Recopiladora

(continuación)

Que la música dentro de sus progra-
mas mejore en calidad y variedad,
pero especialmente en la alegría de
cantar.

Hettie G. Smith

Sussex Camp-fire Opening
(Part Song)

England
Music and words by
Mary C. Chater
Spanish words by R. E. A.
de Reyes and A. Martinez

1

Canción de Nuestra Cabaña

Lentemente con espressione

Mexico

1. En la be - lla Cuer - na - va - ca en un
1. 'Neath the grand Si - er - ra Ma - dre On a

va - lle_en Mé - xi - co, se_en - cuen - tra Nues - tra Ca -
plain in Mex - i - co, Lies our beau - ti - ful Ca -

ba - ña,_un lu - gar lle - no de sol.
ba - ña,— Where Girl Scouts and Guides go.

Più allegro

Va - mos a Nues - tra Ca - ba - ña go -
Oh, come then to see the moun - tains, The

za - re - mos al lle - gar de_a - mis - tad y de_a - le -
cac - tus and sun - ny skies; Hear the crick - et in the

ritard.

grí - a y de be - lle - za sin par.
eve - ning and see the white moon a - rise.

La letra de esta canción se debe a las participantes de la primera sesión Juliette Low en Nuestra Cabaña en el año 1957.

Written by the girls attending the first Juliette Low Session, Our Cabaña, July 1957.

2

2. Cada día_en Nuestra Cabaña
   trabajamos por cumplir
   los ideales del Guidismo
   y de nuestro Fundador.
   Vayamos a la Cabaña
   nuestra promesa_a vivir
   con nuestras hermanas Guías
   la_amistad a compartir.

2. When you see the warm red roofs
   You think of hearts that glow with
        cheer,
   And the walls of sturdy stone work
   Stand for friendship so dear.
   Each day there is filled with
        laughter,
   Each evening is filled with song,
   And our stay in Our Cabaña
   Gives us memories life-long.

3. When we go to Our Cabaña
   We will find ourselves at home;
   There's a greeting smile so friendly
   And a handshake so warm.
   So come now to Our Cabaña
   World friendship to increase,
   And carry to your homeland
   International peace.

A version of this song in the key of G
can be found on page 52.

Our Chalet Song

1. Arriba en la montaña
   Se encuentra un gran Chalet;
   Su techo acogedor
   Abrigará nuestra amistad,
   Venid O Guías venid a él,
   Venid a vuestro hogar.

   Arriba en la montaña
   Se encuentra un gran Chalet;
   Ahí podréis gozar,
   Tendréis trabajo y libertad,
   De vida limpia y pura
   Ahí podréis gozar.

1. High up, high on the mountain,
   We've founded our Chalet.
   Its sloping roof and wide
   Shall shelter us without a care
   And each Girl Scout and Guide
   Shall find a welcome there.

2. High up, high on the mountain,
   We'll go to our Chalet;
   Our simple life is free,
   Our hearts are light, our songs are
        gay,
   We ever shall remember
   The joys of our Chalet.

3. High up, high on the mountain,
   We've founded our Chalet;
   And this its dedication
   Shall never fail nor be undone:
   Each race, each creed, each nation,
   Beneath its roof are one.

In all the verses, the first two lines are
   repeated.

La letra en francés fue escrita para la
   Sesión de Apertura de Nuestro Chalet
   en Adelboden en 1932 y desde
   entonces ha sido adoptada como la
   Canción del Chalet.

The music of this song can be found in
Our Chalet Song Book and various
other Girl Scout/Guide publications.

English version by Betty Askwith

3

Swinging Along

Gladys Jacobs
U.S.A.
Spanish by R. E. A. de
Reyes and A. M. Martinez

Swing - ing a - long the o - pen road,
Por la ve - re— da_al ca - mi - nar,

Swing - ing a - long____ the o - pen road, un - der a
Por la ve - re____ da_al ca - mi - nar, ba - jo_es - te

Swing - ing a - long un - der a sky that's clear.
Por la ve - reda ba - jo el cie - lo_a - zul.

sky that's clear. Swing - ing a -
cie____ lo_a____ zul. Por la ve -

Swing - ing a - long the o - pen road.
Por la ve - re - da_al cam - i - nar.

long____ the o - pen road, In the
re____ da_al ca - mi - nar, Siento la

All in the fall, in the fall of the year. Swing - ing a -
Sien - to la bri - sa la bri - sa del mar. Es la ver -

fall of the year. Swing - ing a -
bri - sa del mar. Es la ver -

Taken from *Girl Scout Pocket Songbook*.
Used by permission.

long, swing - ing a - long, swing - ing a - long the o - pen road,
dad, es la a - mis - tad es el a - mor que sien - to yo—

long, swing - ing a - long, swing - ing a - long the o - pen road,
dad, es la a - mis - tad es el a - mor que sien - to yo—

All in the fall of the year.
Es la a - le - gría de vi - vir.

All in the fall of the year.
Es la a - le - gría de vi - vir.

Alleluia Amen
(Two-part Round)

Con spirito

1.
Al - le - lu - jah, Al - le - lu - jah,

2.
A _____ men, A _____ men.

Cuando el segundo grupo cante su último "Amen," el primer grupo se les une cantando las dos notas altas como están escritas en el último compás. Esto hace que el final sea fuerte y armonioso.

As the second group sings the final "Amen," the first group joins in, singing the two upper notes as written in the last bar/measure. This provides a strong, harmonious ending.

5

A la Puerta del Cielo

Descant and English
version by A. D. Zanzig

Descant for Verse 2

2. A los ni - ños Dios ben - di — ce, y
2. God will bless them so peace - ful - ly sleep - ing, And

1. A la puer - ta del cie - lo ven - den za - pa — tos,
1. At the gate of Heav'n lit - tle shoes they are sell - ing.

a las ma - dres Di - os las a - sis - te,
help the mo - thers whose love they are keep - ing.

Pa - ra los an - ge - li - tos que_an - dan des - cal - zos.
For the lit - tle bare - foot - ed an - gels there dwell - ing.

Coro

Duér - me - te, ni - ño,__ Duér - me - te, ni - ño,
Slum - ber, my ba - by, Slum - ber, my ba - by,

Chorus

Duér - me - te, ni - ño, Duér - me - te, ni - ño,
Slum - ber, my ba - by, Slum - ber, my ba - by,

Duér - me - te, ni - ño, a rru,__ a__ rru.
Slum - ber, my ba - by, a rru,__ a__ rru.

Duér - me - te, ni - ño, a__ rru, a__ rru.
Slum - ber, my ba - by, a__ rru, a__ rru.

2. A los niños que duermen Dios ben -
   dice.
   A las madres que velan Dios las
   asiste.
                    (Coro)

2. God will bless the children so
   peacefully sleeping,
   God will help the mothers whose
   love they are keeping.
                    (Chorus)

Esta encantadora canción de cuna está
dentro del alcance de muchas voces
jóvenes, pero para evitar esfuerzo,
entónenla en tono de Re.

This delightful lullaby does lie within
the compass of many young voices
but, to avoid strain, pitch in key D.

Camp-fire Opening

Australia
Aboriginal
Words by Anne Dreyer
Music by Robin Wood

Con ritmo deliberato

Sit round the camp-fire now night is here,
All birds are rest-ing, No-one is near. Clap with your
hands and tap with your feet, Now sway oh so gent-ly,
keep with the beat. Oh___ Ai Ai Oh___
Ai, Oh___ Ai Ai Oh___ Ai.

Movimientos.
1. Aplaudir. 2. Zapatear.
3. Mecerse.

Actions
1. Clap. 2. Tap. 3. Sway.

Reproduced by permission of the publishers,
  Messrs D. Davis and Co., Ltd.,
  Melbourne.

Barges

Legato

Source Unknown

Out of my win-dow look-ing in the night, I can see the bar-ges' flick-er-ing light; Si-lent-ly flows the ri-ver to the sea, And the bar-ges too go si-lent-ly.

Chorus

Bar-ges, I would like to go with you, I would like to sail the o-cean blue. Bar-ges, have you treas-ures in your hold? Do you fight with pi-rates brave and bold?

Desde mi ventana puedo ver las luces de las barcas en el río. ¿Llevarán tesoros? ¿Serán piratas preparados para luchar? ¡Como me gustaría navegar en ellas!

2. Out of my window looking in the night
I can see the barges' flickering light;
Starboard shines green and port is glowing red,
You can see them flickering far ahead.

(Chorus)

8

Alleluia
(Eight-part Round)

Con spirito   France

Al - le - lu - jah, Al - le - lu - jah, Lou -

anges à Dieu, Al - le - lu - jah.

Alabanzas a Dios   Praises to God

Hambani Kahle
(Zulu Parting Song)

Africa
Arranged by D. Bird
Spanish words by M.L.A.

Go well and safe - ly, Go well and safe - ly
Que te va - ya ,bien,___ Que te va - ya bien,___

Que te va - ya bien,___ etc.

Go well and safe - ly, The Lord be ev - er with you.
Que te va - ya bien,___ Que Dios te_a - com - pa - ña - rá.

2nd verse: Stay well___, etc.

From EYC Songbook, copyright © 1962 World
Around Songs, Inc. Used by permission.

English by Olcutt Sanders

Boysie

Soave

Trinidad and Tobago
Traditional

1. All me day ah work, me day ah work for Boy - sie_____.

All me day ah work me day ah work for Boy - sie._____

Go up town, go down town, see Boy - sie dere,

Go up town, go down town, see Boy - sie dere,

All me day ah work, me day ah work for Boy - sie,

All me day ah work, me day ah work for Boy - sie_____.

Un arrullo de una chica a su enamorado, trabaja para él todo el día; le lee en voz alta para entretenerlo; hasta lo mece en su hamaca. A pesar de esto él es perezoso y no se interesa.

This is a lullaby sung by a girl to her lover. She works all day for him, reads aloud to entertain him, and even rocks his hammock. Despite this, he remains lazy and unhelpful.

All me life ah give, me life ah give for Boysie.
All me life ah give, me life ah give for Boysie.
Sleep Boysie, dream Boysie, till morning come.
Sleep Boysie, dream Boysie, till morning come.
All me life ah give, me life ah give for Boysie
All me life ah give, me life ah give for Boysie.

Alouette

Allegretto

Canada

A - lou - et - te, gen - tille, A - lou - et - te,

A - lou - et - te, je te plu - me - rai.

Solo *Chorus*

Je te plu - me - rai la tête, je te plu - me - rai la tête,

Chorus *Solo* *Chorus* *D.C.*

Et la tête, et la tête, A - lou - ette, A - lou - ette, Oh!

2. Le bec. 3. Le nez. 4. Le dos. 5. Les pattes. 6. Le cou.

Después del primer verso repítase este compás con las palabras al revés: por ej. el último verso como sigue: et le cou, et les pattes, et le dos, et le nez, et le bec, et la tête. Oh Alouette.

As this song proceeds, the third bar/ measure from the end is repeated to include all the parts of the bird already mentioned but in reverse order; i.e., et le cou, et les pattes, et le dos, etc.

Bon Appetit

France

Bon a - , bon a - , bon ap - pe - tit.

"Bon appetit" se traduce "Buen apetito."

"Bon appetit" is a well-known French phrase to wish people a happy meal.

Benedicamus Domino

Be - ne - di - ca - mus Do - mi - no, De - o gra - ti - as.

Gelobet
(Three-part Round)

Giojoso   **Germany**

1. Ge - lo _____ bet sei, Ge - lo _____

bet sei Der Herr mein Gott **2.** Ge - lo _____

bet sei, Ge - lo _____ bet sei,

Der Herr mein Gott. **3.** Ge - lo - bet, Ge - lo - bet, Ge -

lo _____ bet sei, Der Herr mein Gott.

La letra quiere decir: Alabado sea el Señor mi Dios.

The words mean: Praised be the Lord, my God.

Used by permission. From *A.B.C. of Camp Music* by Janet E. Tobitt.

Buon Giorno
(Three-part Round)

Allegro

Italy

Buon gior-no mi-a ca-ra, Bam-bi-na, Mol-te ba-ci! Buon

gior-no mi-a ca-ra, Bam-bi-na, Mol-te ba-ci! Buon

gior no mi-a ca-ra, Bam-bi-na, Mol te bu ci!

La letra quiere decir: "Buenos días, niña querida. Muchos besos para ti!"

The words mean "Good morning, little one. Many kisses to you!"

Los Pollitos

Guayaquil, Ecuador
Traditional

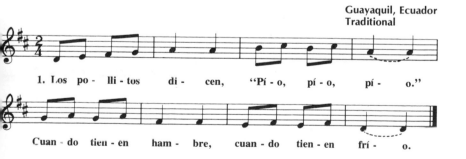

1. Los po-lli-tos di-cen, "Pí-o, pí-o, pí-o."

Cuan-do tien-en ham-bre, cuan-do tien-en frí-o.

2. La gallina busca el maíz y_el trigo para su comida, y les presta_abrigo.

3. Bajo sus dos alas, acurrucaditos. Hasta_el otro día duermen los pollitos.

Little chicks say "pio, pio" when they are hungry or cold. The hen looks for corn, and beneath her wings the chicks sleep till the next day.

Click Go the Shears

Sciolto Australia

Down by the pen, the old shear-er stands,

Grasp-ing his shears in his thin bon-y hands

Fixed is his gaze on a blue-bell-ied joe,

Glor-y if he gets her, won't he make the ring-er go?

Refrain

Click! go the shears, boys, click! click! click!

Wide is his blow, and his hands move so quick. The

ring-er looks a-round and is beat-en by a blow, And

curs-es the old snag-ger with the blue bell-ied joe

blue-bellied joe—a sheep with little wool on it that can be sheared quickly; the ringer —the fastest shearer of the shed; snagger—a slang term for an old 'down-and-out' man.

From the *Australian Campfire Song Book*. Used by permission.

El granjero observa cuidadosamente a cada una de las ovejas que viene a ser esquilada. El ruido de las tijeras se escucha constantemente.

The old shearer watches carefully every sheep that comes to be shorn. The "click, click" of the shears is continually heard.

2. Out on the floor in his cane
     bottomed chair
   Is the boss of the board with his
     eyes everywhere,
   Notes well each fleece as it comes
     to the screen,
   Paying strict attention if it's taken
     off clean.
        (Refrain)

3. The tar-boy is there and a-waiting in
     demand,
   With his blackened tar-pot and his
     tarry hand;
   Sees one old sheep with a cut on his
     back,
   Here's what he's waiting for "Tar
     here, Jack!"
        (Refrain)

El Canto de la Promesa

Letra del Padre Juanito
Garcia Artola
El Salvador

Allegretto

En - tre las Guí - as pro - me - tí Ser - vir al Se -

ñor y lo pri - me - ro pa - ra mí se_ rá el ho -

nor y siem pre mi pro - me - sa

he de_ cum - plir. Ho - nor, leal - tad, no -

ble_ za has - ta_ mo - rir.

15

All Night, All Day

Spiritual
U.S.A.

All night, all day, An - gels watch - in' o - ver me, my Lord. All night, all day. An - gels watch - in' o - ver me____.

Now I lay me down to sleep, An - gels watchin' o - ver me, my Lord. Pray the Lord my soul to keep, An - gels watch - in' o - ver me.

**Toda la noche, toda el día me velan
ángeles. Si duermo, si muero, que el
Señor guarde mi alma.**

2. If I die before I wake, Angels
   watchin' over me, my Lord.
   Pray the Lord my soul to take,
   Angels watchin' over me.
   (Chorus)

3. If I live for ever and a day, Angels
   watchin' over me, my Lord.
   Pray the Lord guard me alway,
   Angels watchin' over me.
   (Chorus)

Auld Lang Syne

Espressivo

Scotland
Words by Robert Burns

1. Should auld ac - quain - tance be for - got And nev - er bro't to mind? Should auld ac - quain - tance be for - got, And days of auld lang syne?

Chorus

For auld lang syne, my dear, For auld lang syne; We'll tak' a cup o' kind - ness yet, For auld lang syne.

The following is sung by Latin American Guides as a closing song.

¿Por Qúe Perder Las Esperanzas?

1. ¿Por qúe perder las esperanzas de volverse a ver?
¿Por qúe perder las esperanzas si hay tanto querer?
(Coro)
No es mas que un hasta luego,
No es mas que un breve adiós,
Muy pronto junto al fuego nos
Nos reunirá el Señor.

2. Con nuestras manos enlazadas en torno al calor
Formemos esta noche un círculo de amor.
(Coro)

2. And here's a hand my trusty friend;
And gie's a hand o' thine;
We'll tak' a cup o' kindness yet,
For auld lang syne.
(Chorus)

17

Land of the Silver Birch

Con espressione

Canada
Arranged by John Cozens

1. Land of the sil-ver birch, home of the beav-er,

Where still the might-y moose wan-ders at will.

Refrain

Blue lake and rock-y shore, I will re-turn once more,

Boom di-di eye di, Boom di-di eye di, Boom di-di eye di boom.

Nostálgicamente.

Tierra del abedul de plata, casa del castor y del alce, voy a regresar a la laguna azul y a la orilla rocallosa. En la llanura siento nostalgia por las colinas del norte. Mi canoa va a traerme tan rápido como un pez y cerca del lago azul construiré mi casa.

*Una segunda voz puede comenzar el coro aquí como un eco.

*Second part enters here, giving the effect of an echo.

Used by permission.

2. My heart is sick for you here in the lowlands,
   I will return to you, hills of the north.

3. Swift as a silver fish, canoe of birch bark,
   Thy mighty waterways carry me forth.

4. There where the blue lake lies I'll set my wigwam,
   Close to the water's edge, silent and still.

18

Bamboo Fiah

Allegro

Guyana

Bam - boo fi - ah is a hot, hot, fi - ah, Bam - boo fi - ah mek so!

Bam - boo fi - ah is a hot, hot, fi - ah, Bam - boo fi - ah mek so!

Oh, Bam - boo fi - ah mek so!

Oh, Bam - boo fi - ah mek so____! Oh, Bam - boo fi - ah

mek so____! Oh, Bam - boo fi - ah mek so____!

Esta canción nos dice que el bambú produce un buen fuego. Pueden agregarse versos extra, como por ejemplo sobre el olmo que produce mucho humo.

This song tells us that bamboo gives a very hot fire. Extra verses could well be added, e.g., Elm-tree 'fiah' is a smoky 'fiah,' etc.

Acompañen con instrumentos de percusión.

Try a percussion accompaniment.

From *Selected National and Folk Songs of Guyana* compiled by Edith Pieters, © 1976. Used by permission.

De Colores

Source Unknown

Con espressione

1. De_____ co - lo - res,_____ de co - lo - res se vis - ten los
1. Oh_____ the col - ours! Oh the col - ours of fields in the

cam - pos en la pri - ma - ve - ra._____ De_____ co -
glit - ter - ing man - tle of spring._____ Oh_____ the

lo - res,_____ de co - lo - res son los pa - ja -
col - ours! Oh the col - ours of birds as they

ri - llos que vie - nen de fue - ra._____ De_____ co -
fly back on shim - mer - ing wing._____ Oh_____ the

lo - res,_____ de co - lo - res es el ar - co
col - ours! Oh the col - ours of rain - bows that

i - ris que ve - mos lu - cir,_____
shine like an arc in the sky_____

Y por e - so los gran - des a - mor - es de mu - chos co -
Of old friend - ships we think and we know that the spring - time will

lo - res me gus - tan a mi.
co - lour those friend - ships a - new.

20

2. De colores, de colores brillantes
  y finos se viste la aurora,
  De colores, de colores son los mil
  reflejos que el sol atesora.
  De colores, de colores se viste el
  diamante que vemos lucir,
  Y por eso los grandes amores de
  muchos colores me gustan a mi.
  Y por eso los grandes amores de
  muchos colores me gustan a mi.

2. See the colours, see the colours as
  dawn clothes the earth in its
  delicate hue,
  See the colours, see the colours that
  glow as the sun rises out of the
  blue.
  See the colours, see the colours that
  shine from the sides of the
  diamond bright.
  Of old friendships we think and we
  know that the springtime will
  colour these friendships anew.
  Of old friendships we think and we
  know that the springtime will
  colour these friendships anew.

3. Canta el gallo, canta el gallo con
  su quiri, quiri, quiri, quiri, quiri.
  La gallina, la gallina con su cara,
  cara, cara, cara, cara.
  Los polluelos, los polluelos con su
  pio, pio, pio, pio, pa.
  Vaya lio con su quiri, quiri, cara,
  cara, cara, pio, pio, pa.
  Vaya lio con su quiri, quiri, cara,
  cara, cara, pio, pio, pa.

3. Now the rooster, now the rooster
  he sings quiri, quiri, quiri, quiri,
  quiri.
  Now the hen, little hen she joins in
  cara, cara, cara, cara, cara.
  Now the chickens, they keep crying
  with their pio, pio, pio, pio, pa.
  What a fussing with their quiri,
  quiri, cara, cara, cara, pio, pio,
  pa.
  What a fussing with their quiri,
  quiri, cara, cara, cara, pio, pio,
  pa.

W.H.

For Health and Strength
(Four-part Round)

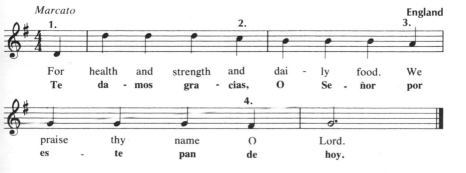

21

El Tren

Allegro

Venezuela

"Pa' Ca - ra - cas" di - ce_el tren cuan - do
"To Ca - ra - cas" says the train when it's

vie - ne de Los Te - ques, "Pa' Ca - Te - ques. Pa' Ca -
chug - ging from Los Te - ques, "To Ca - Te - ques. To Ca -

ra - cas, pa' Ca - ra - cas, siem - pre lle - ni - to de
ra - cas, to Ca - ra - cas, steam a - puff - ing from its

gen - te pa - sa_a ve - ces por un
fun - nel. Al - ways full of peo - ple

tú - nel y_o - tras ve - ces por un puen - te.
trav'ling o - ver brid - ges, thro' a tun - nel.

Esta canción es ideal para improvisar un
juego.

This song is ideal for an improvised
singing game.

2. Cuando pasa por un túnel siempre va
   muy lentamente,
   Cuando pasa por un túnel siempre va
   muy lentamente,
   Con cuidado, despacito para no
   "asusta" a la gente,
   Despacito, despacito caminando,
   lentamente.

2. When it's passing thro' a tunnel it
   goes clanking, slowly clanking;
   When it's passing thro' a tunnel it
   goes clanking, slowly clanking;
   So as not to frighten people travels
   smoothly onward, puffing.
   It takes care to go more slowly,
   always huffing, always chuffing.

22

3. (Cantar rápido, excepto la última línea que es lenta.)

Cuando va por el puente ya comienza
  a acelerar,
Cuando va por el puente ya comienza
  a acelerar.
Corre, corre, corre, corre, ya a
  Caracas va a llegar.
Corre, corre, corre, corre, ya a
  Caracas va a llegar.

3. (Faster, then slower)

When the bridges have been passed,
  then the train begins to hurry;
When the bridges have been passed,
  then the train begins to hurry;
Gets up steam to reach Caracas
  faster, faster, always fast.
Now it's stopping in the station,
  people getting out at last.
                                    H.G.S.

Les Cathédrales Françaises
(Three-part Round)

France

Or - lé - ans, Beau - gen - cy, No - tre Da - me

de Clé - ry, Ven - dô - me, Ven - dô - me.

Esta ronda imita las campanas de un grupo de catedrales localizadas más o menos a 100 kms. al sureste de París. La bella estatua de madera blanca de Nuestra Senora de Cléry se encontró en el siglo XIII cerca del lugar donde está ahora la iglesia dedicada a ella. El rey Luis XI le tenía tal reverencia que mandó hacer figuritas de ella, para usarlas colgadas en su sombrero. El rey Luis XI fué enterrado en esa iglesia.

This round imitates the bells of a group of cathedrals located about 75 miles southwest of Paris. The beautiful white wooden statue of the Madonna of Cléry was found in the 13th century near the present site of the church named after her. Louis XI had such a reverence for this Madonna that he had little figures of her made to wear around his hat, and he was buried in her church.

Footnote taken from *Sing Together*.
Used by permission.

Canción del Campamento

Allegretto

Helena y Elsa Diggs
Argentina

1. Aun - que el sol   que - me con sus ra -
1. Come to   camp,   who minds the weath - er

yos, Aun - que la llu - via - cai - ga sin ce - sar____
Oh? Grey tho' the skies are,   we enjoy the show - ers____.

Aun - que el vien - to   so - ple hura - ca - na -
Come to   camp,   work - ing to - gether

do y ha - ga pe - no - so nues - tro ca - mi - nar
in wind or in sun - shine,   hap - pi - ness is ours.

Es el or - gu - llo   de to - da Guí - a
Then when the sun sets,   our work is ov - er,

estar siem - pre lis - ta   pa - ra ser - vir__
gath - ered to - geth - er   round the camp - fire,

Cuan - do te - ne - mos   di - fi - cul - ta - des
Voic - es up - lift - ed,   mo - ments of mag - ic,

La   ley nos man - da can tar y   re - ír.
Flick - er - ing fire - light our hearts   in - spire,

24

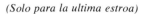

(Solo para la ultima estroa)

To - da tris - te - za se_ol - vi - da - rá.
Flick - er - ing fire - light our hearts in - spire.

2. Nuestra vida_en el campamento
Es gran maestra de privaciones,
Una carpa y un baño modesto
Poca comida_y muchas ilusiones.
La colchoneta puesta_en el suelo
Es nuestro lecho para dormir,
Pero no_importa porque_a la Guía
La Ley le manda cantar y reír.

3. Hay que hachar leña para_el día
Traer el agua del manantial,
Mientras unas hacen la comida
Las otras convierten la carpa_en un
   hogar,
Y cuando_el sol llega_a su ocaso
Nuestro fogón nos reunirá
Y_a las primeras chispas del fuego
Toda tristeza se_olvidará.
Toda tristeza se_olvidará.

Dona Nobis Pacem
(Three-part Round)

Moderato

Source Unknown

1.
Do - na no - bis pa - cem, pa - cem,

do - na no - bis pa - cem.

2.
Do na no - bis pa - cem, do - na no - bis

3.
pa - cem. Do - na no - bis

pa - cem, Do - na no - bis pa - cem.

Danos la paz.   Give us peace.

25

Girl Scouts Together

Words and music by
Gladys Cornwall Goff
U.S.A.

Con moto

Girl Scouts to - geth - er, That is our song,
Guí - as can - te - mos nues - tra can - ción.

Wind - ing the old trails, rock - y and long.
Por las mon - ta - ñas y sob - re el mar,

Learn - ing our mot - to, liv - ing our creed.
Cump - lien - do u - ni - das nues - tra mi - sión.

Girl Scouts to - geth - er in ev - 'ry good deed.
Díos, pat - ria, cre - do, vi - vir y a - mar.

Girl Scouts to - geth - er, Hap - py are we;
Guí - as u - ni - das siem - pre can - tad,

Friend - ly to neigh - bors far o'er the sea;
Brin - dan - do di - cha, a - mor y a - mis - tad,

Faith - ful to coun - try, loy - al to home,
Nues - tra es - tan - dar te en al - to lle - vad,

Known as true Girl Scouts where ev - er we roam.
No ol - vi - dar nun - ca nues - tra buen - a ac - ción.

26

Lord, Let Thy Light So Shine

English words by
Elizabeth Hartley
Spanish words by
Maria Laura Aviña

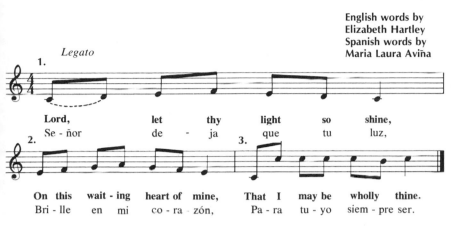

Legato

1.

Lord, let thy light so shine,
Se - ñor de - ja que tu luz,

2. **3.**

On this wait - ing heart of mine, That I may be wholly thine.
Bri - lle en mi co - ra - zón, Pa - ra tu - yo siem - pre ser.

God Has Created a New Day

Words and Music by
Marie Gaudette
U.S.A.

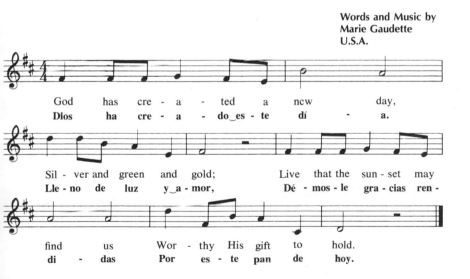

God has cre - a - ted a new day,
Dios ha cre - a - do es - te dí - a.

Sil - ver and green and gold; Live that the sun - set may
Lle - no de luz y a - mor, Dé - mos - le gra - cias ren -

find us Wor - thy His gift to hold.
di - das Por es - te pan de hoy.

Pongan especial atención a la melodía en
los compases 2 y 3, ya que con
frecuencia se canta incorrectamente.

Take special care with the tune in bars
2 and 3 as all too often these are
sung incorrectly.

Linstead Market

Jamaica

1. Car - ry me ack - ee go a Lin - stead Mar - ket,
Not a quat - tee wut sell! Car - ry me ack - ee go a
Lin - stead Mar - ket, Not a quat - tee wut
sell! Lawd, what a life, not a bite,
What a Sa - tur - day night! Lawd, what a
life, not a bite, What a Sa - tur - day night!

Llevo mi "ackee" al mercado de
Linstead. Pregono "ackee" que va
bien con arroz pero la gente toca las
frutas y no compra nada.

2. Everybody come feel up, feel up,
   not a quattee wut sell!
   Everybody come feel up, feel up,
   not a quattee wut sell!
   (Chorus)

ackee—una fruta roja; quattee—moneda
pequeña; feel up—tocar.

ackee—a red fruit; quattee—a small
sum of money; feel up—touch.

Esta canción se puede acompañar con
instrumentos de percusión.

This song needs a drum
accompaniment to give full effect to
the rhythm.

I Let Her Go, Go

Marcato

Trinidad and Tobago

I let her go, go, Ee ay I let her go, go, Ee ay I let her go_____ I let her go, go, go.

BAILE: Tomen a su pareja y formen un círculo. Pónganse frente a frente y si el círculo es muy grande formen un círculo interior.

A.—Los compañeros bailan uno hacia el otro y al llegar a "go go," palmean con sus manos las del otro.

B.—Den la vuelta y hagan lo mismo con la persona que está detrás.

C.—Otra vuelta para regresar a su propia pareja, palmean de nuevo y paran en "go."

D.—Den un paso a la derecha para continúar con otra pareja.

Como Trinidad es un país muy caluroso, este baile debe ser con movimientos muy suaves y un ligero movimiento de caderas no estaría fuera de lugar.

Take partners and form a single circle, then turn to face partners. (If numbers are large, an inner circle may be needed.)

A. Partners dance up to each other and on 'go go' both clap each other's hands twice.

B. They turn and do the same to the person who is behind.

C. They turn again and dance up to their own partners and clap once, but linger on 'go . . ,'

D. They then pass by the right shoulder and continue with a new partner.

As Trinidad is a very hot country, this dance should be taken in a leisurely manner. A little hip swinging is not out of place.

Jubilate, Deo
(Canon for Six Voices)

C. Praetorius, c. 1600

Ju - bi - la - te, De - o, Ju - bi - la - te, De - o, Al - le - lu - ia!

Australian Hiking Song

Words and music
by A. W. Leadbeater
Australia

When the birds are calling by the blue la - goon, And the breeze keeps whisper - ing a haunt - ing tune. When the stars are winking at the bright new moon, That's the time for hi - king. That's_____ the time for hik - ing.

Chorus

See the Willie Wag - tail oh so gay, See the ba - by mag - pies black and grey, When the bush is calling all the live - long day. That's_____ the time for hi - king.

30

Cuando la naturaleza luce todo su
esplendor, invitándonos a gozar de la
vida, es el momento de salir a
disfrutarla.

2. When the fish are biting in the big
   green pool,
   And the water beckoning so deep
   and cool,
   When you steal away to play the
   wag from school,
   That's the time for hiking.

*Es optativo añadir la segunda voz,
 vocalice donde no hay palabras.

*The second voice is optional, vocalize
 it except where words are shown.

Used by permission of the Girl Guides
Association of Australia.

Haere Mai

Arranged by Hemi Piripata
New Zealand

Moderato

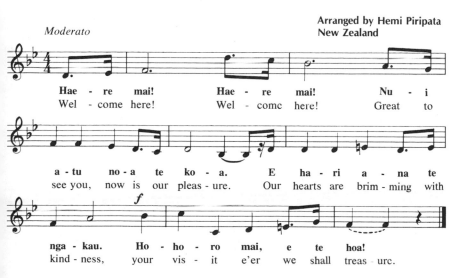

Hae - re mai! Hae - re mai! Nu - i
Wel - come here! Wel - come here! Great to

a - tu no - a te ko - a. E ha - ri a - na te
see you, now is our pleas - ure. Our hearts are brim - ming with

nga - kau. Ho - ho - ro mai, e te hoa!
kind - ness, your vis - it e'er we shall treas - ure.

**Bienvenidas, nos da mucho gusto
tenerlas aquí.**

It's a Small World

Music and words by
Richard M. Sherman and
Robert B. Sherman

1. It's a world of laugh - ter, a world of
En el mun - do hay ri - sas y do-

tears; it's a world of hopes and a world of
lor, Es - per - an - zas y hay tam - bién te-

fears. There's so much that we share that it's time we're a-
mor; Mu - cho hay en ver - dad que po - der com - par-

ware. It's a small world af - ter all.____
tir En - tre la hu - ma - ni - dad.____

It's a small world af - ter all. It's a
Muy pe - que - ño_el mun - do es, Muy pe -

small world af - ter all. It's a small world
que - ño_el mun - do es, De - be_ha - ber más

af - ter all, It's a small, small world.____
her - man - dad, Muy pe - que - ño es.____

2. **Una luna hay**
   Sólo hay un sol,
   Para todos brillan
   Sin distinción.
   Y_aunque muy grandes son
   Las montañas y_el mar
   Muy pequeño el mundo es.

2. There is just one moon
   And one golden sun
   And a smile means friendship
   To ev'ryone.
   Though the mountains divide
   And the oceans are wide
   It's a small world after all.

Lili Gal

Traditional
Guyana

Soave

Li - li Gal, Li - li Gal, Li - li Gal, Li - li Gal, wha' mek yo' bra - zen so?

Li - li Gal, Li - li Gal, Li - li Gal, Li - li Gal, wha' mek yo' bra - zen so? Me

come out - a fo' - teen, gan in - to fif - teen, dah mek me bra - zen so! Me

come out - a fo' - teen, gan in - to fif - teen, dah mek me bra - zen so!

Todos sabemos lo importante que es tener quince años. Por eso no debemos sorprendernos que 'Lili Gal' presuma tanto.

'Lili Gal' is feeling bold because she has reached fifteen years of age. Substitute other "feelings" to add to verses, e.g., "happy" instead of "brazen."

From *Selected National and Folk Songs of Guyana* compiled by Edith Pieters © 1976. Used by permission.

De-ci, De-la, Semons la Joie
Jubelana

Music and French words by
Marcelle de Meulemeester

Refrain *Moderato*

De - ci de - là se mons la joie,
Ju - be - la - na let us re - joice

Un pe - tit grain de joie. De - ci de - là
Guides all o - ver the world. Ju - be - la - na

don - nons d'la joie, A ceux qui n'en ont pas.
come raise your voice, Let our song be heard.

Verse

1. A ceux qui train - ent, souf - frent et pein - ent, à
1. Far and near, come let us share,

ceux que la hai - ne at - tend de main.
send - ing a mes - sage of cour - age and joy.

Donne et par - tage le tout vieux mes - sage der -
Sor - row will van - ish, dark clouds be ban - ished

rière les nu - ages se cache un ciel bleu.
When our song ech - oes all o - ver the world.

English words by Marjorie Grant and
Mrs. Cowan-Douglas, South Africa,
for a Baden-Powell Jubilee Camp,
1957.

Used by permission of Marcelle de
Meulemeester.

34

2. Barre sur ta route soupçons et doutes
   Mets en déroute, chagrins et cafard.
   Jette la semence de paix,
   d'espérance.
   Amour et confiance lèveront bien
   demain.

2. For by tomorrow, you'll want to
   follow
   The path that was shown us so long
   ago
   With wisdom he gave us our vision
   and made us
   United in friendship all over the
   world.

Vem Kan Segla?

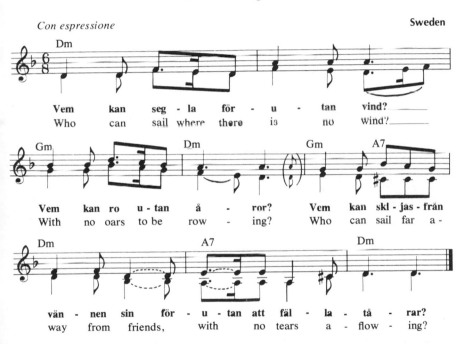

Con espressione

Sweden

Vem kan seg - la för - u - tan vind?
Who can sail where there is no wind?

Vem kan ro u - tan å - ror? Vem kan skl - jas - från
With no oars to be row - ing? Who can sail far a -

vän - nen sin för - u - tan att fäl - la - tå - rar?
way from friends, with no tears a - flow - ing?

2. Jag kan segla förutan vind
   Jag kan ro utan åror.
   Men ej skiljas från vännen min
   Förutan att fälla tårar?

2. I can sail where there is no wind
   With no oars to be rowing.
   But I can't sail far away from
   friends
   With no tears a'flowing.

   H.G.S.

Cuesta decir adiós a los amigos sin
derramar lágrimas.

Used by permission Scoutförlaget,
Stockholm.

Second part added by B. Pulliam.

35

Lullaby

Con espressione

Bahamas

Hush lit - tle ba - by don't you cry._____ You know your Ma - ma was born to die;_____ All my tri - als, Lord,_____ soon be o - ver._____ Too late, my broth - ers_____ Too late, _____ but nev - er mind;_____ All my tri - als, Lord,_____ soon be o - ver._____

2. Jordan's river is chilly and cold
   It chills the body but not the soul.
   Chorus

3. There is a tree in Paradise
   And seekers call it the tree of life.
   Chorus

**Al arrullar la madre a su niño
  refliexiona en las penas y alegrías de
  la vida.**

The mother croons to her baby and
  reflects on the sorrow and happiness
  in life.

36

Kookaburra

Marion Sinclair
Australia

Vivace

1. Koo - ka - bur - ra   sits   on   an   old   gum   tree,
2. Mer - ry, mer - ry King of the   bush is   he____, Laugh, Koo - ka - bur - ra,
3. laugh,   Koo - ka - bur - ra,   Gay   your   life   must   be.

Kookaburra tiene una risa singular y es también capaz de matar serpientes. El "gum tree" es el eucalipto.

Kookaburra has an uncanny "laugh." He is capable of killing snakes. The "gum tree" is the eucalyptus.

Used by permission. Girl Guides Association of Australia.

Maleyla

Source Unknown
Africa

Ma - ley - la,   ma - ley - la,   ma - ley - la,____   Ma - ley - la,
ma - ley - la, ma - ley - la____   ____Ma - ley - la,   ma - ley - la,   ma - ley - la,
Ma - ley - la,   Ma - ley - la,   ma - ley - la,   ma - ley - la____.

From *The Australian Campfire Song Book.* Used by permission.

Old Gaelic Melody

Moderato
Descant

p

Traditional Tune
Descant by Douglas Coombes

Ah ————— ,

Ah ——————— ,

Melody

Ah ——————— ,

Ah —————— .

The well-known words of this beautiful melody can be found in *Songs for Canadian Girl Guides* under "Thanks for a Day" (or in your memory). They are suitable for flag ceremonies and many other occasions.

Morning Is Here

Source Unknown

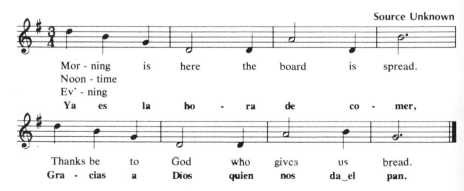

Mor - ning   is   here   the   board   is   spread.
Noon - time
Ev' - ning

Ya   es   la   ho - ra   de   co - mer,

Thanks be   to   God   who   gives   us   bread.
Gra - cias   a   Dios   quien   nos   da_el   pan.

Mi Chacra

Vivace

Argentina

1. Ven - gan a ver mi cha - cra que es her - mo - sa;
1. Come now and see my farm which is so beau - ti - ful.

Ven - gan a ver mi cha - cra que es her - mo - sa.
Come now and see my farm which is so beau - ti - ful.

El po - lli - to ha - ce a - sí: ki - ki - rí;
Lit - tle chickens go like this: kee kee ree,

El po - lli - to ha - ce a sí: ki - ki - rí. O
Lit - tle chickens go like this: kee kee ree. O

pas, ca - ma - rade, O pas, ca - ma - rade, O pas, O pas, O pas; O
come now my friend, O come now my friend, O come, O come, O come; O

pas ca - ma - rade, O pas ca - ma - rade, O pas, O pas, O pas.
come now my friend, O come now my friend, O come, O come, O come.

2. El perrito hace así: guau - guau.

2. Little puppies go like this: bow - wow.

3. El gatito hace así: mi - au.

3. Little kittens go like this: miaow.

4. El burrito hace así: ji - jo

4. And the donkey goes like this: hee - haw.

5. El patito hace así: cua - cua.

5. Little ducklings go like this: quack - quack.

6. El chanchito hace así: oinc - oinc.

6. Little piglets go like this: oink - oink.

39

Peace

Words by Glendora
Gosling
Music by Viola Wood
U.S.A.

Peace I ask of thee, O riv - er, Peace, peace,
Paz te pe - di - mos oh rí - o, paz, paz,

peace. When I learn to live se - rene - ly
paz. Cuan - do ya lle - gó la no - che

Cares will cease. From the hills I gath - er cour - age,
des - can - sad. ba - jo las lin - das es - tre - llas

Vi - sion of the day to be, Strength to lead and faith to
u - ni - das por la_a - mis - tad ve - mos el dí - a que

fol - low, All are giv - en un - to me.
lle - ga lle - nas de fe - li - ci - dad.

Peace I ask of thee, O riv - er, Peace, peace, peace.
Paz te pe - di - mos oh rí - o paz paz paz.

Used by permission.

I Listen and I Listen

Words and music by
Hazel Charlton
Arranged by
Douglas Coombes

Giojoso

In the morn - ing ear - ly I go down to the sea And see the mist on the shore. I lis - ten and I lis - ten.

2. When I
3. When the
4. And at

4. lis - ten, I lis - ten And I lis - ten.

Cuando estoy cerca del mar ya sea con tempestad o con calma, escucho la voz de Dios que me habla.

2. When I go to the rocks I go looking for shells,
And feel the sand beneath my feet,
I listen and I listen.

3. When the stormy day comes, waves crash on the cliffs
And the wind whistles through my hair. I listen and I listen.

4. And at night when I sleep and the sea is calm,
The gentle waves lap the shore. I listen and I listen.

5. I sometimes think that God is talking to me
When I hear the sound of the sea. I listen and I listen.

Sangam Song

Comdr. Japheth

The sym - bol of one - ness, San - gam is our pride where
love and af - fect - ion don't change like the tide. Re -
gard - less of co - lour, re - li - gion or creed, To
spread be - ne - vo - lence we're sow - ing the seed.
Guides of all na - tions, to - ge - ther we stand, In
good - will and friend - ship u - ni - ted our band. To
help the weak and a - ged we make our - selves strong. To
gain in - spi - ra - tion we al - ways sing this song.
San - gam O San - gam. Sym - bol of one - ness.

Used by permission.

Wayfarers Grace

English words by
M. Elizabeth Worsfold
Tune by Canon
G. C. E. Ryley

Moderato

For all the glo - ry of the way, For Thy pro -
A - la - be - mos al Se - ñor De - mos le

tec - tion night and day, For roof - tree, fire — and bed and
gra - cias al Ha - ce - dor; Por el ho - gar — y la_a - mis -

board, For friends and home,___ we thank Thee, Lord.
tad, Grac - ias, Se - ñor,___ A - le - lu - ya.

Reproduced from *Kent County Song Book*
by permission.

Rosen fra Fyn
(Four-part Round)

Andante   **Denmark**

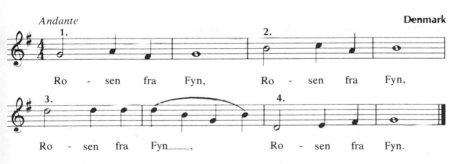

1.   2.

Ro - sen fra Fyn, Ro - sen fra Fyn,

3.   4.

Ro - sen fra Fyn___, Ro - sen fra Fyn.

La letra significa: Rosas de Fyn (la casa
de Hans Christian Andersen en
Dinamarca).

The words mean: Roses from Fyn (the
home of Hans Christian Andersen in
Denmark).

Song Without Words

Allegro

Germany

La - la - la   la   la   la - la la,   la - la   la   la   la   la.

Hol - de - ri   Hol - de - ri - e - di - ri,   Hol - de - ri   cou cou,

Hol - de - ri - e - di - ri,   Hol - di - ri cou   cou,   Hol - de - ri - e - di - ri,

Hol - de - ri   cou cou,   Hol - de - ri - e - di - ri,   Ho!

Una persona puede dirigir la canción e indicar con los dedos cuantas veces se van a repetir los 'cou-cous', lo que causará mucha risa.

Como alternativa, en cada repetición de la canción, el número de 'cou-cous' puede aumentarse cada vez e.j. Verso 2: todas cantan 'cou-cou' dos veces, luego tres y así sucesivamente hasta cansarse.

The leader of the song indicates by her fingers how many times the group is to sing the 'cou-cous.' The result causes much hilarity.

Alternatively increase the number of 'cou - cous' with each verse, e.g. verse 2 sing 'cou-cou' twice, verse 3 sing 'cou-cou' three times etc. until exhaustion sets in.

La parte A.
Las cantantes se mecen en ritmo durante la parte A y su repetición (con las palmas de la mano juntas, tocándose las mejillas alternadamente según se mecen).

Section A
All sway in time (with flattened palms pressed against alternate cheeks).

As contrived by Falk of Our Chalet. Taken from *Girl Scout Pocket Songbook*. Used by permission.

La parte B.
En el primer cómpas se palmean las rodillas con ambas manos rápidamente.

1. Se dan una palmada fuerte en las rodillas.

2. Aplauden.

3. Cierran los puños dejando el pulgar separado y señalando con ellos sobre los hombros hacia atras (más fuertemente en la palabra 'cou-cou'). Se repiten los movimientos 1, 2 y 3 hasta el final.

Section B
First bar, slap knees with both hands rapidly (to make the voice quiver!).

1. Slap knees.

2. Clap hands.

3. Close fists with thumbs out and jerk over shoulders (especially hard on word 'cou-cou'). Repeat 1, 2 and 3 motions to the end.

Why Shouldn't My Goose?
(Four-part Round)

U.S.A.

Why should-n't my goose Sing as well as thy goose When I paid for my goose, Twice as much as thou?

Los cantores se sientan en los talones y se levantan cuando cantan 'goose' en el tercer compás.

Singers sit on their heels and rise up on to their knees when they sing "goose" in the third bar.

From *The Ditty Bag* compiled by Janet E. Tobitt. Used by permission.

45

El Tortillero

Con amore

Chile

No - che obs - cu - ra, na - da ve - o
In the dark - ness I see noth - ing,

Pe - ro lle - vo mi fa - rol____ Por tus
Tho' I raise my lan - tern high.____ On your

puer - tas, voy pa - san - do, y can -
door - step I am wait - ing, With a

tan - do con a - mor,____
song of love I sigh.

Chorus

Mas____ voy can - tan - do____ Con
Loud____ tho' I'm sing - ing,____ My____

____ har - ta pe - na,____ Quien com - pra mis__ tos - ta -
____ heart is ach - ing. Come buy my fresh tos - ta -

i - tas, Tor____ ti - llas bue - nas
i - tas. Tast____ y tor - ti - llas.

2. Bella_ingrata, no respondes
A mi grito placentero.
Cuando pasa por tu casa,
Pregonando_el tortillero.
(Coro)

2. Oh ungrateful, not to answer
When I give my hopeful cry.
As I linger on your doorstep,
'Hot tortillas come and buy,'
(Chorus)

46

3. Ya me voy a retirar con
   Mi canasta y farol
   Sin tener tú compasión
   De_este pobre tortillero.
          (Coro)

3. But I see now, I must leave you,
   Take my basket and my light,
   For no pity you have shown me
   So I'll sing a sad goodnight.
                    H.G.S.
          (Chorus)

Rondo de las Estaciones

Allegro ma non troppo   Panama

1.
La be - lla pri - ma - ve - ra de ver - de se vis -
The love - ly, love - ly Spring - time has clothed her - self in

tió. La be - lla pri - ma - ve - ra de ver - de se vis -
green. The love - ly, love - ly Spring - time so beau - teous to be

2.
tió, Vió_a_o - to - ño con in - vier - no bai - lan - do_el ri - go -
seen. She sees the Fall and Win - ter join in a hap - py

dón. Bai - lar no qui - so_es - tí - o y di - jo so - ca -
dance, But Sum - mer who re - fus - es looks at them all a -

3.
rrón: ¡Dan - zad! ¡Dan - zad! Que me so - fo - co
skance. Dance on! Dance on! While I en - dure the

yo. ¡Dan - zad! ¡Dan - zad! Que me so - fo - co yo.
sun. Dance on! Dance on! En - joy the sea - son's fun.

                                    H.G.S.

Navajo Happy Song

Marcato

American Indian

Hi yo, hi yo ip si ni yah, Hi yo,

hi yo ip si ni yah, Hi yo hi yo ip si ni yah,

Hi - yo, hi yo ip si ni yah. Ip si ni YAH!

La letra no significa otra cosa que 'tra - la - la' y la canción se canta en fiestas y otras ocasiones alegres. Cántese toda 3 veces añadiendo los últimos dos compases al final; el último 'Yah' se grita.

This song is sung at feasts and joyous occasions, the words having no specific meaning. Sing it three times and shout the final 'Yah.'

Grabada por Marguerite Twohy en Nuevo Mexico.

As recorded by Marguerite Twohy in New Mexico.

Taken from the *Girl Scout Pocket Songbook.* Used by permission.

Lu-la-le

Con movimento

Source Unknown

L R L R L

Lu - la - le, lu - la - le, Lu - la - lu - la - le, Lu - la,

R L R L R L R

Lu - la, Lu - la, Lu - la - lu - la - le, ___ Lu - la - le, Lu - la - le,

Lu - la - lu - la - le,   Lu - la,   Lu - la,   Lu - la - le.

L = balanceo a la izquierda.	L = sway left.
R = balanceo a la derecha.	R = sway right.

This is a good international song. It can be sung several times, one of the group calling out the name of a different country each time. The singing is louder or softer depending on whether the country is far or near.

Footnote from *The Canadian Jubilee Song Book*. Used by permission.

Canción Mundial

The World Song

1. Marchemos todas con decisión
   En pos de nuestro ideal,
   Y prometamos siempre servir
   En un mundo fraternal.
   Y que nuestras voces resuenen
   Allende los montes y el mar,
   Para unir nuestra fe, nuestro amor
   En un solo canto universal.

1. Our way is clear as we march on,
   And see! our flag on high
   Is never furled throughout the world,
   For hope shall never die!
   We must unite for what is right
   In friendship true and strong,
   Until the earth in its rebirth
   Shall sing our song! Shall sing our song!

2. Bien alta la bandera levantad,
   Y que libre al viento ondee,
   Cual símbolo de nuestra lealtad
   Y esperanzas que no mueren.
   Y que nuestras manos se enlacen bien,
   Formando amistosa cadena
   Para unir nuestro amor, nuestra fe
   En el cumplimiento de nuestra ley.

2. All those who loved the true and good
   Whose promises were kept,
   With humble minds, whose acts were kind,
   Whose honour never slept.
   These were the free and we must be
   Prepared like them to live,
   To give to all both great and small
   All we can give, all we can give.

Música de Sibelius. Derechos registrados. Prohibida su reproducción. De venta en oficinas Nacionales de las Guías/Scouts.

The music of this song is by Sibelius. It is copyrighted and may not be reproduced. It is on sale at Girl Guide and Girl Scout national headquarters.

Letra en Español Placido de Montoliu.

English words by Gavin Ewart

49

I'm a Dandy

Vivo
Verse

Traditional
Barbados

1. See my lit - tle brown girl, Call she for me,

call she for me, call she for me, You

see my lit - tle brown girl, call she for me,

Chorus

'cos I want to go home. O you may walk, An' you may

talk, But you can tell__ by__ my style an' my

fash - ion, By my high - stand - ing

col - lar, an' my ties to mul - ti - ply, I'm a

dan - dy I'm__ a dan - dy, I'm__ a dude___.

Este caballero muy bien vestido está muy orgulloso de su presencia, y espera que su novia esté siempre muy elegante.

This well-dressed "dandy" is very proud of his appearance. He expects his "girl friend" to be just as smart as he is.

Used by permission.

2. When I'm out in high company
High company, high company,
My girl must be a lovely to see
Or I leave she alone.
(Refrain)

3. If you see me out on a spree
Out on a spree, out on a spree,
Every thing just right you'll agree
'Cause I do set a tone.
(Refrain)

El Coquí

Leggiero

Puerto Rico

El co - quí, el co - quí a mi me en can - ta,
The co - quí sings a lul - la - by - soft - ly,

Es tan lin do el can - tar del co - quí,
I can hear the co quí all night long;

Por las no - ches al ir a a - cos - tar - me.
Though I fall fast a - sleep when it's bed - time,

Me a - dor - me - ce can - tan - do a - sí: ¡Co -
In my dreams comes his sweet lit - tle song: Co -

quí! ¡Co quí! ¡Co - quí - quí - quí - quí! ¡Co -
kee! Co - kee! Co - kee - kee - kee - kee! Co -

quí! ¡Co - quí! ¡Co - quí - quí - quí - quí!
kee! Co - kee! Co - kee - kee - kee - kee!

English by Olcutt Sanders. Courtesy of
World Around Songs, Burnsville,
North Carolina.

Coquí (co-kee)—frog

51

Las Mañanitas

Con espressione

Mexico

Es - tas son las ma - ña - ni - tas que can -
With a morn - ing song we greet you as King

ta - bael Rey Da - vid, Pe - ro no e - ran tan bon -
Da - vid used to sing, But more beau - ti - ful than

Fine

i - tas co - mo las can - tan a - quí.
his song is the mu - sic we bring.

Coro

Des - pier - ta, mi bien, des - pier - ta, mi -
Wake up, then, O my - lov - ed, Wake

ra que ya a - ma - ne - ció, Ya los pa - ja - ri - llos
up for the dawn is nigh; The birds are sweet - ly

D.C. al Fine

can - tan, la lu - na ya se me - tió.
sing - ing, The moon has gone from the sky.

The above is a fine example of a folk "aubade," a song sung at dawn. It is often used as a birthday morning greeting.

From *The Ditty Bag,* compiled by Janet E. Tobitt. Used by permission.

Johnny Appleseed

Con spirito

Spanish words from Uruguay

The Lord is good to me, And so I thank the Lord, - For
Dios se‿a - cor - dó de mi, Y‿a El le a - gra - dez - co. Por -

giv - ing me the things I need, The sun, the rain, and the
que me dió El pan de hoy, Y llu - via y sol, Fru -

ap - ple - seed. The Lord is good to me.
to y flor, Dios se‿a - cor - dó de mí.

Dios se acordó de mí,
Y‿a El le agradezco
Porque me dio
Un corazón
Y‿así amar su creación,
Dios se‿acordó de mi.

2. And every seed that grows
   Shall grow into a tree.
   And one day soon
   There'll be apples there
   For everyone in the world to share.
   The Lord is good to me.

Rise Up, O Flame

Fermato

C. Praetorius, c. 1600

1. 2. 3. 4.

Rise up, O flame By thy light glow - ing.
Prén - de - te lla - ma, con - tu luz lle - na.

5. 6. 7. 8.

Show to us beau - ty, vi - sion and joy.
A nues - tras al - mas con a - mis - tad.

ay be sung in up to eight parts at a
bar's distance.

This grace may be sung to the above
tune in the same manner.

May God supply the wants of my
  brother,
And give to me a truly thankful
  heart.

sed by permission of Möseler Verlag,
Wolfenbüttel und Zürich.

53

Love Is Come Again

Translated by J. M. C. Crum,
Tune, French Traditional

Allegretto con amore

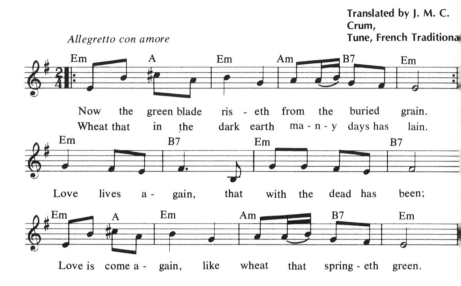

Now the green blade ris - eth from the buried grain.
Wheat that in the dark earth ma - n - y days has lain.

Love lives a - gain, that with the dead has been;

Love is come a - gain, like wheat that spring - eth green.

Como el trigo crece del grano sembrado en el campo, de la misma manera nuestro Señor resucitó de entre los muertos. Que nuestros corazones respondan al amor y se alcen por encima de nuestra tristeza.

2. In the grave they laid Him, Love
    whom men had slain,
   Thinking that never He would rise
    again:
   Laid in the earth like grain that
    sleeps unseen,
   Love is come again, like wheat that
    springeth green.

3. Forth He came at Easter, like the
    risen grain,
   He that for three days in the grave
    had lain.
   Quick from the dead my risen Lord
    is seen;
   Love is come again, like wheat that
    springeth green.

4. When our hearts are wintry,
    grieving or in pain,
   Thy touch can call us back to life
    again.
   Fields of our hearts that dead and
    bare have been;
   Love is come again, like wheat that
    springeth green.

Words from *Oxford Book of Carols,*
reprinted by permission of Oxford
University Press.

Shalom Chaverim

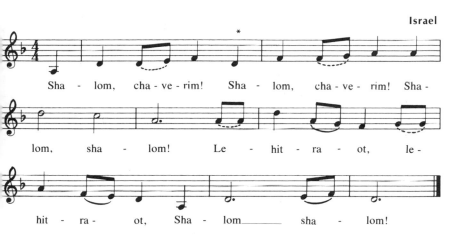

Israel

Sha - lom, cha - ve - rim! Sha - lom, cha - ve - rim! Sha -
lom, sha - lom! Le - hit - ra - ot, le -
hit - ra - ot, Sha - lom____ sha - lom!

Traemos la buena nueva, paz en la
tierra a los hombres de buena
voluntad.

Glad tidings we bring of peace on
earth,
Goodwill toward men.
Of peace on earth, of peace on earth,
Goodwill toward men.

Las voces pueden entrar sucesivamente.
Puede cantarse con hasta 8 partes.

*Succeeding voices enter. May be sung
in up to 8 parts.

English by A. D. Zanig

Camp Grace

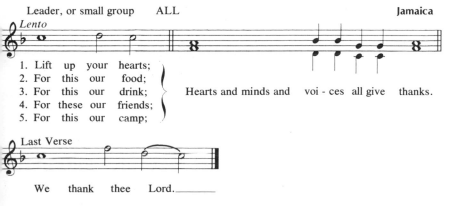

Jamaica

Leader, or small group   ALL

Lento

1. Lift up your hearts;
2. For this our food;
3. For this our drink;
4. For these our friends;
5. For this our camp;

Hearts and minds and voi - ces all give thanks.

Last Verse

We thank thee Lord.____

Adapted from a Jamaican folk song.

Quietly

Soave con movimento

Words and music by S. Stevens

1. Qui - et - ly in the morn - ing, Qui - et - ly when dawn is near, Qui - et - ly in the sun - rise, Qui - et - ly God is there.

Chorus

List - en for God in qui - et - ness, List - en and you may hear. List - en for God in still - ness, List - en for God is there.

En el silencio escuchamos la voz de Dios.

2. Quietly in the springtime,
   Quietly when leaves appear,
   Quietly in the greenness,
   Quietly God is there.
   (Chorus)

3. Quietly in the evening,
   Quietly when stars appear,
   Quietly in the stillness,
   Quietly God is there.
   (Chorus)

4. Quietly we are gathered,
   Quietly for night is near,
   Quietly close beside us,
   Quietly God is there.
   (Chorus)

Cielito Lindo

Allegretto   Mexico

1. De   la   Sie — rra   Mo - re - na,   Ci_e — li - to
1. From the Sie — rra   Mo - re - na,   Ci_e — li - to

Lin - do   vi_e — nen   ba - jan - do
Lin   do   comes — light - ly   danc - ing. ___

Un   par   de_o - ji - tos   ne - gros,   Ci_e - li - to
Black eyes   shin   ing   with   laugh - ter   Ci_e - li - to

Lin - do,   de - con - tra - ban - do. ___
Lin - do,   she's   so   en - tranc - ing. ___

Coro

¡Ay,   ay,   ay,   ay!   can - ta_y   no
Ay,   ay,   ay,   ay! ___   Sing,   do   not

llo - res, ___   Por - que can - tan - do   se_a - le - gran, Ci_e -
sor - row. ___   For   hap - pi - ness - comes   from sing - ing, Ci_e -

li - to   Lin - do,   los ___   co - ra - zo - nes ___ .
li - to   Lin - do   brigh - tens   the   mor - row ___ .

2. Ese lunar que tienes
   cielito lindo
   junto a la boca,
   no se lo des a nadie
   cielito lindo
   que a mí me toca.
          (Coro)

3. Una flecha en el aire
   cielito lindo
   lanzó cupido,
   y como fué jugando
   cielito lindo,
   yo fuí el herido
          (Coro)

57

Hevenu Shalom Aleichem

Marcato

Israel

He - ven - u Sha - - lom a - lei - chem, He - ven - u
With words of peace now we greet you, With words of

Sha - - lom a - lei - chem, He - ven - u Sha -
peace now we greet you, With words of peace

lom a - lei - chem, He - ven - u Sha - lom, Sha - lom,
now we greet you, We bring you greet - ings, greet - ings,

1. 2. etc.

Sha - lom a - lei - chem.
greet - ings of peace.

Last time

Sha - lom a - lei - chem.
Greet - ings of peace.

La canción se empieza despacio hasta terminar a gran velocidad. Las palmadas acompañan este ritmo de aceleración. Añadir la parte superior para el clímax final. Alegría, amor, alabanza, etc. pueden substituir a "paz," según convenga.

Clap the first beat in every bar (x). Take the song slowly the first time, then increase the speed until a very fast rate is reached, with clapping as indicated. Add upper part for a last time climax.

Joy, love, praise etc. could be substituted for 'peace' to suit various occasions.

Shalom significa 'Paz' y también se utiliza para decir 'Hola' o 'Adios'.

Shalom means "Peace" and is also used for "Hello" and "Goodbye."

T.I.R.O.

Giocoso

Source Unknown

De pie en un círculo, uniendo los brazos por la espalda. **Poner el pie derecho cruzando el pie izquierdo de tu compañera.** Todo el círculo se balancea de izquierda a derecha al compás de la música; en los 'Os' se inclinan hacia adelante y se doblan hacia atrás. Comenzar muy lentamente y cantarlo tres veces y hacerlo más a prisa poco a poco y moviéndose más hacia dentro y hacia afuera.

L = hacia la izquierda. **R** = hacia la derecha.

F = hacia adelante. **B** = se doblan hacia atrás.

Stand in a circle, linking arms behind backs. Place your right foot across the left foot of your neighbour. The whole circle sways left and right in time to the music; at the "Os" you bend forwards and backwards. Begin rather slowly and sing it three times, getting gradually quicker, and swinging further in and out.

L = sway left. **R** = sway right.

F = lean forward. **B** = lean back.

As far as we know, the letters have no significance.

Hello! Hello!

E. O. Harbin
U.S.A.

1. Hello! 2. Hello! 3. Hello! 4. Hello! We are glad to meet you.
Se - an bien - ve - ni - das.

We are glad to greet you. Hello! Hello! Hello! Hello!
Se - an bien - ve - ni - das.

Para cantarse en cuatro grupos. El primer grupo empieza y sostiene su "Hello" hasta que los demás grupos hayan cantado sus "hellos". La última serie de "hellos" se sostiene dejando que la armonía gradualmente desaparezca.

The first group holds its "hello" until the other three groups have sung theirs. Hold the last group of "hellos" until the chord quietly dies away.

Today Is a New Day

Words and music by
P. Feltham
Spanish words by M. L. A.

Allegretto

To - day is a new day, So
Hoy es un nue - vo dí - a, A -

let us re - joice, And praise the Lord who
le - gré - mo - nos, De - mos gra - cias al

made it, With heart and mind and voice.
cie - lo, con to - do_el co - ra - zón.

Used by permission.

Himno Guia

Mexico

Por ha - ber - nos da - do la luz de tu sol,

el a - zul del cie — lo que es nues - tro co - lor

u - ni - das las Guí - as te a - la - ba - mos hoy

y jun - tas de - ci - mos, gra - cias Se - ñor.

2. Por nuestras juntas y por la_amistad
Que entre nosotras siempre reinará.
Todas te_ofrecemos nuestra
buena_acción
Y juntas decimos: gracias Señor!

Merci, Seigneur
(Three-part Round)

France

Mer - ci, Seig - neur, Mer - ci, Seig - neur, Mer - ci, Seig - neur.

Gracias à Dios.   Thank you, God.

Lullaby Baby

Tune from Argentina

Soave

Lul - la - by Ba - by, Child di - vine____,

Peace - ful - ly sleep, dear son of mine__.

High a - bove your star shines clear_____.

Lul - la - by Ba - by, Child most dear.

2. Lullaby Baby, manger bed. Gentle
   oxen at Your head.
   Shepherds kneel in silence near.
   Lullaby Baby. Child most dear.

3. Lullaby Baby, King of kings. All
   the world with gladness sings.
   Kings will seek to find You here.
   Lullaby Baby, Child most dear.

When I Needed a Neighbour

Con sentimento

Words and music by Sydney Carter

When I need - ed a neigh - bour, were you there, were you there? When I need - ed a neigh - bour, were you there? And the creed and the col - our and the name won't mat - ter, were you there?

Como en la parábola del buen Samaritano la pregunta es ¿trataremos de ayudar a nuestro prójimo?

2. I was hungry and thirsty, were you there, were you there? . . .

3. I was cold, I was naked, were you there, were you there? . . .

4. When I needed shelter, were you there, were you there? . . .

5. When I needed a healer, were you there, were you there? . . .

6. Wherever you travel I'll be there, I'll be there, Wherever you travel I'll be there.

Jesus, Jesus, Rest Your Head

John Jacob Niles
Arranged by D.B.
U.S.A.

Este villancico nos cuenta que Jesús
nació y durmió en un pesebre, mien—
tras que los viles duermen en colchón
de plumas.

To that manger came the wise men,
Bringing things from hin and yon.
For the mother and the father
And the blessed little Son.
Milkmaids left their fields and flocks
And sat beside the ass and ox.

65

Hey, Hey, Hey, Jubilee Hey

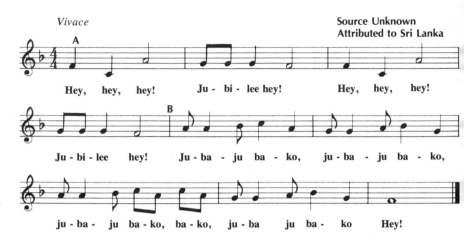

Vivace

Source Unknown
Attributed to Sri Lanka

A

Hey, hey, hey! Ju - bi - lee hey! Hey, hey, hey!

B

Ju - bi - lee hey! Ju - ba - ju ba - ko, ju - ba - ju ba - ko,

ju - ba - ju ba - ko, ba - ko, ju - ba ju ba - ko Hey!

Las figuras B1 - B2 - B3 y B4 son el coro y deben repetirse después de cada una de las A.	The figures B1, B2, B3, and B4 are a chorus and must be repeated after each A section.
Ejemp.: Se canta A1 y enseguida todas B; A2 y todas las B; etc.	Example: Sing A1, then do all of B; sing A2, then do all of B; etc.

A1 Hey, hey, hey!	*Jubi - lee hey!*	*A2 Hey, hey, hey*	*Jubi - lee hey!*
Aplaudan 3 veces a la derecha.	**Aplaudan 3 veces a la izquierda.**	**Truenen los dedos con los brazos a la derecha. (3)**	**Truenen los dedos con los brazos a la izquierda (3)**

3 claps right.	3 claps left	3 'finger snaps' right	3 'finger snaps' left
Repeat	**Repitan**	**Repeat**	**Repitan**

A3 *Hey, hey, hey!*

**Truenen los dedos
con los brazos
en alto.**

3 high snaps

Repitan

Jubi - lee hey!

**Truenen los dedos
con los brazos
abajo.**

3 low snaps

Repeat

$$A4 = A1 + A2 + \begin{pmatrix} \text{a la derecha} \\ \text{y} \\ \text{a la izquierda} \end{pmatrix}$$

$$A4 = A1 + A2 + \begin{pmatrix} \text{to the right} \\ \text{and} \\ \text{to the left} \end{pmatrix}$$

B1 *Ju - ba - ju*   *ba-*   *ko*

Palmoteen las rodillas   **Aplaudan**   **Truenen los dedos . . .**   **Aplaudan**

Slap knees   Clap   Snap fingers   Clap

B2 *Repitan B1*   *Repeat B1*

B3 Ju-ba-ju　　　　　　　*ba-ko*　　　　　*ba-ko*

B4 Ju-ba-ju　　　　　　　*ba-ko*

hey!

68

Zulu Lullaby

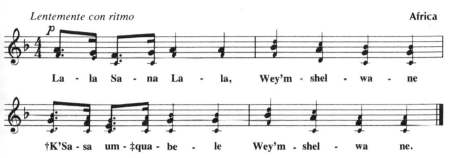

Lentemente con ritmo
p
Africa

La - la Sa - na La - la, Wey'm - shel - wa - ne

†K'Sa - sa um - ‡qua - be - le Wey'm - shel - wa - ne.

†K pronounced Goo. ‡q has a click.

N.B. It is important that the melody dominates.

Reproduced from the *Kent County Song Book* with permission.

Taps

Tempo rigoroso

Day is done, Gone the sun, From the
Des - can - sad to - do es paz cae la

sea, from the hills, from the sky. All is
no - che en la tie - rra y el mar des - can -

well. Safe - ly rest. God is nigh.
sad que el Se - ñor cer - ca es tá.

The word "Taps" was originally applied to the tapping on a drum, which in the American Army was the signal to retire. When later the bugle was used, the call retained its original name.

Words used by permission of Widener University (formerly Pennsylvania Military College).

Daylight Version (requested by the World Chief Guide)

Thanks and praise for our days
'Neath the sun, 'neath the stars,
'neath the sky.
As we go, this we know:
God is nigh.

69

Jamaica Farewell

Calypso tempo **Words and music by Irving Burgie**

Down the way where the nights are gay and the
sun shines dai - ly on the moun - tain top
I took a trip on a sail - ing ship And when I
reached Ja - mai - ca I made a stop. But I'm

Chorus
sad to say, I'm on my way,
Won't be back for man - y a day. My
heart is down, My head is turn - ing a - round, I had to
leave a lit - tle girl in Kings - ton town.

2. Sounds of laughter ev'ry where and
   the dancing girls swaying to and
   fro,
   I must declare, my heart is there,
   Tho' I've been from Maine to
   Mexico,
   But I'm . . .
   (Chorus)

3. Down at the market you can hear
   ladies cry out while on their
   heads they bear
   Ackey rice, salt fish are nice, and
   the rum is fine any time of year.
   But I'm . . .
   (Chorus)

Zum Gali Gali

Folk Song
Israel

A la marcia

1. He - cha - lutz   le'   -   man   a - vo - dah,

Chant

Zum   ga - li,   ga - li,   ga - li,   zum   ga - li,   ga - li.

A - vo - dah   le'   -   man   he - cha - lutz

Zum   ga - li   ga - li,   ga - li,   zum   ga - li,   ga - li.

1. The pioneer's purpose is work.

2. He - cha - lutz le'man ha - b'tu - lah,
   Ha - b'tu - lah le'man hechalutz.

2. The pioneer is for his girl.

3. Ha shalom le'man ha - a - mim, Ha -
   a - mim le'man ha shalom.

3. Peace is for all nations.

Un grupo canta el segundo y tercer
versos mientras el otro grupo continúa
con el 'chant'. Los dos grupos pueden
alternar el canto de los versos y el
'chant'.

One group continues singing verses 2
and 3, while the other maintains the
chant. The two groups should change
for alternate verses.

Pasión

Words by Roberto Arce
Music by
Perion Aceredo J.
Costa Rica

Con moto

Yo te llevo en el pe - cho co - mo u - na per - li - ta

ga - ta que a - dor - na - ron los in - dios al na - cer la luz del

al - ba. Te en - con - tra - ron can - tan - do en u - na

rús - ti - ca ca - ba - ña pues tu pa - dre fue

un vie - jo tro - va - dor de la mon - ta - ña.

Coro

Zum - ba que zum - ba ma - rim - ba—
Zum - ba - ba zum - ba ma - rim ba—

en mi co - ra - zón aun - que se rom - pan las
On my heart you play E'en tho' your keys are all

Fine

te - clas que son de fin - o co - yol,
bro - ken You know what I wish to say.

H.G.S.

2. Cuando_estabas chiquilla y
   juguetona_allá_en el rancho
   Te mimaban los indios que te
   querían tanto tanto.
   Tus canciones nacieron en las jícaras
   del campo.
   Y hoy vagan alegres en el orbe sacro
   santo.

   (Coro)

3. Yo te llevo_en el alma virgencita
   soñadora
   Te abandonó tu padre cual si fueras
   pecadora.
   Te dejó sin bautizo traicionando
   tu_ilusión,
   Y por eso te_han dado el dulce
   nombre de Pasión.

   (Coro)

This tuneful song does not translate
easily; however, it is a good idea to
vocalize the verse and then join in
the chorus.

World Hunger Grace

Con movimiento

Music by Rev. Robert I. Crocker

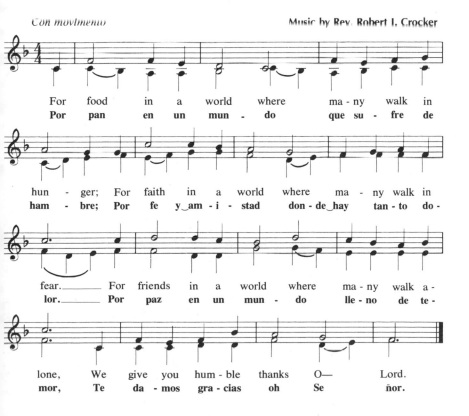

For food in a world where ma - ny walk in
Por pan en un mun - do que su - fre de

hun - ger; For faith in a world where ma - ny walk in
ham - bre; Por fe y_am - i - stad don - de_hay tan - to do -

fear._____ For friends in a world where ma - ny walk a -
lor._____ Por paz en un mun - do lle - no de te -

lone, We give you hum - ble thanks O— Lord.
mor, Te da - mos gra - cias oh Se ñor.

Music by permission of the Reverend Robert
J. Crocker.

Used by Hunger Task Force, Anglican
Church, Diocese of Huron.

73

Slumber, Slumber

English words by
M. Louise Baum
Spanish words by
R. E. A. de Reys and
A. M. Martinez
Music by Arthur B. Targett

2. Slumber so peacefully, slumber so
happily,
Lifted beyond the blue.
Where in the starlight the moon is a
boat,
Quietly carrying you.

Tutú Marambá

Traditional
Brazil

Con tenerezza

Tu - tú ma - ram - bá, não ve - nhas mais cá, Que o
Tu tú ma - ram - bá stay far a - way from here, My

pai do me - ni - no te man - da ma - tá; Tu -
child now is sleep - ing, now sleep - ing with - out fear. Tu -

tú ma - ram - bá, não ve - nhas mais cá, Que o
tú ma - ram - bá, I pray you come not near, Or

pai do me - ni - no te man - da ma - ta.
fa - ther will chase you a - way from our dear.

Dor - me en gra - ça - di - nho, pe - que - ni - do da ma - mãe,
Sleep my dear - est lit - tle one, en - wrapt in slum - ber sound.

Que é le é bo - ni - ti - nho e fi - lhi - nho da ma - mãe.
Al - ways be our hap - py child, no dan - ger is a - round.

H.G.S.

Tutú Marambá—el coco—the
bogeyman (Too-*too* mah-rahm-*bah*)

75

Yellow Bird

Haiti
Words by Marilyn Keith
and Alan Bergman
Music by Norman Luboff

Yel - low bird, up high in ba - na - na
tree. Yel - low bird, you sit all a - lone like me. Did your la - dy friend
leave the nest a - gain? That is ver - y sad. make me feel so bad. You
can fly— a - way, in the sky— a - way. You more luck - y than me!

Yel - low bird, up high in ba - na - na
tree. Yel - low bird, you sit all a - lone like me. Bet - ter fly— a - way
in de sky— a - way. Pick - er com - ing soon, pick from night to noon. Black
and yel - low you, like ba - na - na too. They might pick you some day!

76

Verse

1. I al - so— have a pret - ty gal,_____
2. Wish that I— was a yel - low bird,_____

She not with me to - day. They all the same, the
I fly a - way with you. But I am not a

pret - ty gal,_____ make them the nest, then they fly a -
yel - low bird,_____ so here I sit, noth - ing else to

1. way._____
2. do!_____ Yel - low bird,

yel - low bird, yel - low bird._____

El cantante—un plátano—simpatiza con
el pájaro amarillo cuya novia lo acaba
de abandonar. Se compara con él por
el color, pero lo envidia por no poder
volar.

Viva León

Words and music by
Tina Lopez
Nicaragua

Allegretto

Leal San - tia - go de los ca - ba - ller - os_____ Es mi
De mer - ce - des la Vir - gen ben - di - ta_____ Es la

lin - da ciu - dad co - lo - nial_____ Per - fu - ma - da con
gran pa - tron - ci - ta de Le - ón_____ que nos dio la mu -

los pe - be - ter - os_____ de tu impo - nen - te y_an -
jer mas bo - ni - ta_____ pa - ra que fuer - a a -

ti - gua Ca - te - dral_____ El Po - cho - te es_su Fuen - te Cas -
dor - no_en mi re - gión_____ Es Subti - a - va la_in - di - ge - na

ta - lia_____ don - de me - na se fué a_in - spi - rar
jo - ya_____ con que León se_acos - tum - bra_ata - viar

don - de pu - so Ru - bén su san - da - lia_____ pa - ra con
y la play - a de su Po - ne - loy - a_____ es co - mo

glo - rias al mun - do des lum - brar_____ Por to - do_el
un cielo ten - di - do jun - to_al mar_____

o - ro del mun - do_____ no cam - bia - ría a mi

78

León____ pues lo quiero con a - mor - pro - fun - do

y es el ce - re - bro de to - da mi na - ción____ ____!

León pue - de ser a - ba - ti - do pe - ro nun - ca ven -

(grito)

ci - do, ¡Viva León querido!

I love my beautiful city of León. It is
the heart of the nation. Viva León
for ever!

Herr, Bleibe Bei Uns

Legato

Germany

Herr, blei - be bei uns, Denn es wird A - bend
Ben - dí - ce - nos, Se - ñor, Al ter - mi - nar el

wer - den, Der Tag hat sich ge - nei - get.
dí - a, To - do_en si - len - ci - o du_er - me.

From *Our Chalet Song Book,* used with
permission.

Abide with us, O Lord, for it is now
   the evening.
The day is past and over.

A Grace
(Two-part Canon)

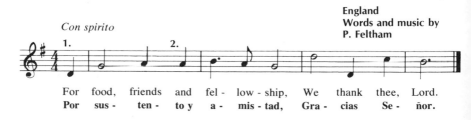

England
**Words and music by
P. Feltham**

Con spirito

For food, friends and fel - low - ship, We thank thee, Lord.
Por sus - ten - to y a - mis - tad, Gra - cias Se - ñor.

Used by permission.

Posadas (Christmas celebrations)

These celebrations, which date from the 16th century, are called Posadas (or lodgings) and begin on December 16th, continuing for nine days. They commemorate the journey of Joseph and Mary to Bethlehem and their nightly search for somewhere to stay.

Each night a different house is offered as the Posada; a procession is formed with children carrying the figurines of Mary on a donkey and Joseph with the angel behind. Everyone carries candles or lanterns and sings song number 1 until they reach the closed doors of the chosen house. Outside the closed doors, the group stops and asks in song for the lodgings.

The words and tunes of the songs differ from state to state, as can also the procedure.

Posada 1
Mientras se Camina de una Estación a Otra
While Walking from One Station to the Other

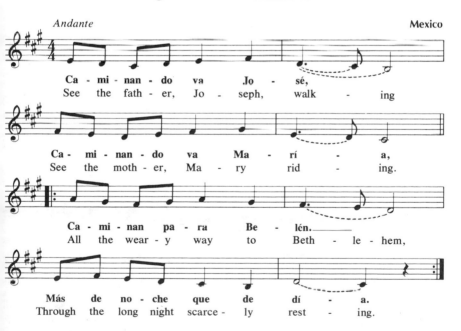

Andante · Mexico

| Ca - mi - nan - do va Jo - sé, |
| See the fath - er, Jo - seph, walk - ing |

| Ca - mi - nan - do va Ma - rí - a, |
| See the moth - er, Ma - ry rid - ing. |

| Ca - mi - nan pa - ra Be - lén. |
| All the wear - y way to Beth - le - hem, |

| Más de no - che que de dí - a. |
| Through the long night scarce - ly rest - ing. |

Los caminantes divinos,
De las almas despreciados,
Andan por esos caminos
Llorosos y fatigados.
Andan por esos caminos
Llorosos y fatigados.

See these pilgrims poor and humble,
No one gives them aid or shelter,
So fatigued they only stumble,
Blindly o'er the darkened way.
So fatigued they only stumble
Blindly o'er the darkened way.

H.G.S.

81

Posada 2
Para Pedir Posada

En nom - bre del cie ____ lo,
In - the name of Heav ____ en.

Os pi - do - po - sa ____ da Pues no
Give, oh give us shel ____ ter. My dear

pue - de an ____ dar mi es -
wife no far - ther can go. We are ex -

po - sa a - ma ____ da.
haust - ed, we fal ____ ter, fal ____ ter.

Spanish version

Posada 2 (Fuera) verses 1 and 2 are sung requesting entrance, but the owner of the house refuses, singing verses 1 and 2 (Dentro). Everyone continues to other doors singing song 1 as they walk, repeating the request and the refusal with verses 3 and 4. At verses 5 and 6 (Fuera), the 'landlord' realizes the importance of his guests and admits them amidst great rejoicing, verses 5 and 6 (Dentro). At this point, he sings the third song. After a prayer, and possibly carols (such as the carol on page 85), there follow refreshments and finally the breaking of the Piñata.

English version is self-explanatory with regard to Posada 2.

VERSOS PARA PEDIR POSADA

Fuera

1. En nombre del cielo
   Os pido posada,
   pues no puede andar
   Mi esposa amada.

2. No seas inhumano
   Tennos caridad
   Que el Dios de los Cielos
   Te lo premiará.

3. Venimos rendidos
   Desde Nazareth
   Yo soy carpintero
   De nombre José.

4. Posada te pide
   Amado casero
   Por sólo una noche
   La Reina del Cielo.

5. Mi esposa es María
   Es reina del Cielo
   y madre va a ser
   del Divino Verbo.

6. Dios pague señores
   Vuestra caridad
   Y que os colme el cielo
   de felicidad.

VERSOS PARA DAR POSADA

Dentro

1. Aquí no es mesón
   Sigan adelante
   Yo no puedo abrir
   no vaya a ser un tunante.

2. Ya se pueden ir
   Y no molestar
   Porque si me enfado
   Los voy a apalear.

3. No me importa el nombre
   Déjenme dormir,
   Pues que ya les digo
   Que no hemos de abrir.

4. Pues si es una Reina
   Quién lo solicita
   ¿Cómo es que de noche
   anda tan solita?

5. ¿Eres tú José?
   ¿Tu esposa es María?
   Entren peregrinos
   no los conocía.

6. ¡Dichosa la casa
   Que abriga este día
   a la Virgen pura,
   La hermosa María!

VERSES TO ASK FOR SHELTER

(Outside)
In the name of Heaven,
Give, oh give us shelter.
My dear wife no farther can go,
We are exhausted, we falter, falter.

From distant Nazareth we've come,
My wife is Mary and Joseph's my
    name.
Don't be inhuman, show us you care,
Then God in Heaven will show you the
    same, you the same.

Please kindly landlord once more I
    entreat,
For the Queen of Heaven this night.
Her babe will come to show the world
He is the Prince of peace and light, and
    light.

VERSES TO GIVE SHELTER

(Inside)
Off you go! We have no room,
You must away, so stop talking.
You could be bold robbers,
This door stays shut, so keep walking,
    walking.

It matters not what you both are called,
Leave me to sleep for I'm tired too.
I will not open, get you gone!
If you don't go I will beat you, beat
    you.

Welcome, oh welcome, I knew you
    not.
Virgin most pure come in and rest.
Let us rejoice that God sent you here,
This house of ours is greatly blest,
    greatly blest.

H.G.S.

83

Posada 3
Entren Santos Peregrinos

Traditional
Mexico

Con anima

En - tren San - tos Pe - re - gri - nos, Pe - re -
En - ter in most ho - ly pil - grims, ho - ly

gri - nos, Re - ci - ban es - te rin -
pil - grims, That I may play my

cón, que aunque es po - bre la mo - ra - da, la mo -
part, In ma - king you most wel - come, you most

ra - da, Os la doy de co - ra - zón.
wel - come, In my home and in my heart.

Cantemos con alegría, alegría,
Todos al considerar,
Que Jesús, José y María, ay María,
Nos vinieron hoy a honrar.

Let us sing with hearts and voices,
 hearts and voices,
And observe this wondrous sight,
That here the Holy Fam'ly, Holy
 Fam'ly
Have honoured us tonight.

H.G.S.

Los Pastores a Belén
(Carol)

Giocoso

Source Unknown

1. Los pas - to - res a Be - lén co - rren pre - su - ro - sos,
1. Shep - herds haste to Beth - le - hem, All of them are rac - ing,

Lle - van de tan - to co - rrer los za - pa - tos ro - tos.
Hold - ing high their bro - ken shoes, Bare - foot they go chas - ing.

Coro *pp* < >

Ay, ay, ay, que_a - le - gres van, ay, ay, ay, si
Ay, ay, ay, let's hap - py be, ay, ay, ay, let's

vol - ve - rán, con la pan, pan, pan, con la
run and see, with a tam, tam, tam, with a

f

de, de, de, con la pan, con la de, con la
bour, bour, bour, with a tam, with a bour, with a

pan - de - re - ta y las cas - ta - ñue - las.____
tam - bour - ine and all the cas - ta - nets.____

2. Un pastor se tropezó
   A media vereda.
   Y un borrequito gritó,
   "Este aquí se queda."
   (Coro)

2. One poor shepherd he fell down
   Sprawling on the pathway.
   Little lamb called out in fun,
   "He has come but halfway!"
   (Chorus)

H.G.S.

La Piñata

Traditional
Mexico

Da - le, da - le, da - le, No pier - das el ti - no.
Hit it, hit it, hit it! Hold - ing tight the stri - ker.

Mi - de la dis - tan - cia, Que_hay en el ca - min - o.
Meas - ure well your dis - tance, Aim at the piñ - a - ta!

A piñata is a clay jar covered with gay colored crêpe paper in the shape of some animal, bird, flower, or something attractive. It is filled with candies, popcorn, nuts, or small party favors, and is hung by a cord from the ceiling or the branch of a tree. The players each in turn are given a stick and, with eyes blindfolded, try to break it. Finally, someone breaks the piñata, the contents are scattered, and all the players scramble for them.

From *Brownies Around the World*, Book 1, published by Girl Guides of Canada/Guides du Canada.

Ira Congo

Con espressione

Africa

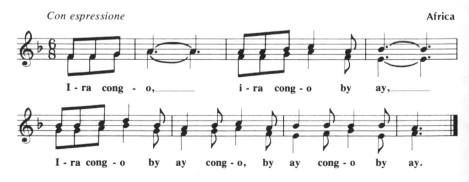

I - ra cong - o,_____ i - ra cong - o by ay,_____

I - ra cong - o by ay cong - o, by ay cong - o by ay.

From *Canadian Jubilee Song Book*. Used by permission.

La Sanjuanerita

Guatemala
L. y M. de Guadalupe
Hernández

Yo soy in - di - ta de San Juan, Mi pue - blo - ci - to_es un jar - dín con flo - res de co - lo - res mil, no sin cla - ve - les y_a - le - li.

Siem - bro la pa - pa siem - bro_el fri - jol ha - go tor - ti - llas pa - ra_el pa - trón mas cuan - do ven - ga fies - ta San Juan,

Se po - ne_a - le - gre mi co - ra - zón, con la ma - rim - ba va - mos bai - lar to - dos con - ten - tos bo - ni - to son.

This Indian girl tells of the joys of
living in San Juan.

La Llorona

Con espressione   Mexico

1. To - dos me di - cen el ne - gro, llo - ro - na, ne -

gro pe - ro___ ca - ri - ño - so,___, Yo

soy co - mo_el chi - le ver - de, llo - ro - na, pi -

can - te pe - ro sa - bro - so.___ Yo ___

Ay de mi! llo - ro - na,___ llo - ro - na de_a

- yer y hoy.___ A - yer ma - ra___

___ vil - la fui -, llo - ro - na, y_a - ho - ra ni som - bra

soy.___ A - yer ma - ra vil - la - fui - llo -

ro - na, y_a - ho - ra ni som - bra soy.___

2. Dicen que no tengo duelo, llorona,
   porque no me ven llorar.
   Hay muertos que no hacen ruido,
      llorona.
   y es más grande su penar.

   Ay de mí, llorona,
   llorona de azul celeste.
   Y aunque la vida me cueste, llorona,
   no dejaré de quererte.

3. Si al cielo subir pudiera, llorona,
   las estrellas te bajara.
   La luna a tus pies pusiera, llorona,
   con el sol te coronara.

This haunting song is difficult to
   translate, but is well worth the effort
   of learning in its present form.

La Palomita

Con grazia

Paraguay

Ya sa len las pa - lo - mi - tas, Per - fu -

ma - das de re - se - da. De ba - jo de la en ra -

ma - da, Ca - da u - na con su ga lán. 2. Que bo -

2. Que bonita es la trigueña
   Y que coqueta ella está
   Que gracio sa la morena
   Y la rubita sin par.

How beautiful the little "doves" look
when dancing with their escorts. One
is dark and vivacious, another
graceful, while the fair one is the
loveliest of all.

Pokare Kare

Maori
New Zealand

Con espressione

1. Po - ka - re ka - re a - na, Nga wai o Ro - to - ru - a,

Whi - ti a - tu koe e hi - ne, Ma - ri - no a - na e.

E hi - ne e, Ho - ki mai ra,

Ka ma - te ah - au i te ar - oh e.

Pronunciación: Wh = f. E siempre es una sílaba por sí misma. Tuhi = tu - li.

Pronunciation: Wh = f, Nga = na. Au = a - oo, E = é and is always a separate syllable; Aroha = arowa, Tu'i = too - lee.

90

2. Tuhi tuhi taku reta
   Tuku atu taku rungi
   Kei kite to iwi
   Raruraru ai e.
   (Chorus)

3. Kau pau aku pepa
   Kua whati taku pene
   Ke taku aroha
   Mau tonu ana e.
   (Chorus)

Si tienes problemas para pronunciar las palabras de esta canción, puedes tararear o vocalizar. La armonía es muy linda.

If you have difficulty with these words, this song, with its upper part, sounds beautiful when sung to "la" or hummed.

Lullaby from Valencia

Music arrangement and lyrics by Alvin and Josefa P. Mills
Spain

Con tenerezza

Duér - me te ni - ño bo - ni - to____
Close your eyes my lit - tle ba - by____

La la la la la la la la la la

la, Duér - me - te mi_a - mor - con es - ta can - ción____
Joy - ous dreams my love - go to sleep my child____

yo_es - toy jun to_a ti,____ duér - me - te.
close your eyes my love,____ close your eyes.

From *Children's Folk Songs from Spain*,
Pepa's Publishing Studio, Weddington
Street, Van Nuys, California 91401. Used by
permission

Running Game

Con spirito

Source Unknown
Belgium

La   la   etc.

Juego de Bélgica.

Tomen a su pareja y con las demás formen un círculo cojidas de las manos.

1. **Corran 16 pasos a la izquierda y otros 16 a la derecha.**

2. **Enseguida 4 pasos hacia el centro y allí levantar 4 veces las rodillas. - Dar 4 pasos hacia atrás y otra vez en el círculo grande volver a levantar las rodillas 4 veces. - Repetir nuevamente todo el punto 2.**

3. **De cara a la pareja, pongan las manos en la cintura y balanceen lateralmente las piernas 16 veces. Giren media vuelta y repitan con la otra compañera.**

4. **Se repite el 2.**

5. **Se repite el 1.**

¡Alto para un respiro!

Juego de Bélgica

With your partner form a circle, all holding hands.

1. 16 running steps left, 16 to the right.

2. 4 steps towards centre; 4 on the spot with knees up; 4 steps back to place; 4 on the spot with knees up. Repeat 2.

3. Face partner and do 16 "side" steps, hands on waists (*see diagram*). Turn away and do 16 "side" steps to *new* partner.

4. Repeat 2.

5. Repeat 1.

Stop for breath!

Los Maizales

Peru
Folk Song

Los mai - za - les bro - tan con pri - mor

ful - gu - ran sus ho - jas de co - lor; La tie - rra fer - til,

el sol be - só, su be - llo gra - no ger - mi - nó.

Tie - rra Pe - rua - na de_ho - nor te_em - bria - gas.

Después de la faena intelectual
  vamos presurosos a jugar,
Cual nuestros padres al son de pan,
  vamos al campo a cultivar.
Tierra Peruana, de honor te
  embriagas.

This song describes the beauty of the
  cornfields and suggests that all
Peruvians should help with the task
of "growing their bread."

ed by permission of the U.S. Committee
or UNICEF.

O Lê Lê O Bahia

Leggieramente

Brazil

1. Da Ba - hi - á me man - d'ram. O Lê Lê O Ba - hi -
1. There are suit - ors at my door

á. Um ces - ti - nho de ca - já, O Lê Lê O Ba - hi -
Six or eight or may - be more,

á. E man - da - ram per - gun - tar, O Lê Lê O Ba - hi -
And my fath - er wants me wed,

á. Se eu que - ria, me ca - sar. O Lê Lê O Ba - hi -
Or at least that's what he said.

á O Le o La O Lê Lê O Ba - hi - á, O Le O

D.C. Finale

1.
2.

la. O Lê Lê O Ba - hi - á. O Le o á á

2. Eu mandei dizer pra êle
O lê - lê - o Ba - hi - a.
Que queria, mas não já
O - lê - lê - o Ba - hi - a.
Que queria ir à Bahia
O - lê - lê - o Ba - hi - a.
Preparar o enxoval
O - lê - lê - o Ba - hi - a.
(Coro)

2. And I told him that I will,
O - lê - lê - o Ba - hi - a.
When the rivers flow up hill,
O - lê - lê - o Ba - hi - a.
Or the fish begin to fly.
O - lê - lê - o Ba - hi - a.
Or the day before I die,
O - lê - lê - o Ba - hi - a.
(Chorus)

Freely translated from the Portuguese by K. Cartwright.

94

Kom Mee Naar Buiten
The Golden Oriole
(Two-part Canon)

Allegretto

The Netherlands

Kom mee naar bui - ten al - le - maal, Dan
Come to the woods with care - free soul, To

zoe - iten wij de wie - le - wal, En
hear the gold - en Or - i - ole, For

ho - ren wij dien mu - zi - kant, Dan is
if that mins - trel you do hear, You know that

zo - mer weer in't land! Du - del -
sum - mer must be near! Too - ra -

djo klinktzijn lied, Du - del - djo klinktzijn lied. Du - del -
le - o is his song, Too - ra - le - o is his song. Too - ra -

djo en an - ders niet.
le - o he sings all day long.

95

Kyrie
(Three-part Round)

Andante Suriname

Ky - ri - e, Ky - ri - e, e - lei - son,

Ky - ri - e, Ky - ri - e, e - lei - son,

Ky - ri - e, Ky - ri - e, e - lei - son.

Señor, ten piedad. Lord, have mercy on us.

Make New Friends
(Four-part Round)

Moderato U.S.A.

Make new friends but keep the old;
A - mis - tad es lo - que nos u - ne.

One is sil - ver and the oth - er gold.
Y lo que nos ha - ce pro - gre - sar.

Atención: Un error muy común es dejar fuera la nota alta en el tercer compás. Esto quita brillantez a la ronda.

Beware: A common mistake is to leave out the top note (E♭) in bar 3. This takes away the brightness of the round.

Glossary

Italian	English	Spanish
Allegro	quick, lively	alegre, vivo
Allegro ma non troppo	not too quickly	alegre pero no demasiado
Allegretto	moderately fast	moderademente alegre
Allegretto con amore	moderately fast with feeling	moderadamente alegre con amor
A la marcia	in the style of a march	tiempo de marcha
Andante	at a walking pace	al paso
Con amore	with love	con amor
Con anima	soulfully	con sentimiento
Con espressione	with expression	con expresión
Con grazia	with grace	con gracia
Con moto	with movement	con movimiento, movido
Con movimento	with movement	con movimiento
Con ritmo deliberato	with strict rhythm	con ritmo deliberado
Con sentimento	with feeling	con sentimiento
Con spirito	with spirit	con animación
Con tenerezza	with tenderness	con terneza
Fermato	firmly	firmemente
Giocoso	gaily	jocoso
Giojoso	joyously	con alegría
Legato	smoothly	suave, unido
Leggiero	lightly	ligero
Leggieramente	lightly	ligeramente
Lentemente con espressione	slowly with expression	lento con expresión
Lentemente con ritmo	slowly but rhythmically	lento con ritmo
Lento	very slowly	lento
Marcato	with marked rhythm	con ritmo marcado
Moderato	moderate in speed	moderado
Più	more	más
Rallentando (rall.)	getting slower	reduciendo velocidad
Sciolto	freely, easily	libre, fácil
Soave	gently	suave
Soave con movimento	gently with movement	suave con movimiento
Tempo riogoroso	in exact time	a ritmo exacto
Vivace	briskly	vivamente
Vivo	vivaciously	vivo, vivamente

Indice   *Index*